THE WORLD'S MOST
BEAUTIFUL PLACES

CLIVE GIFFORD

Grand Canyon – Toroweap Point at sunrise.

THE WORLD'S MOST
BEAUTIFUL PLACES

CLIVE GIFFORD

President: Sean Moore
Production Director: Adam Moore
Editorial Director: Lisa Purcell

Art Direction and Cover Design: Duncan Youel at
OilOften, London. www.oiloften.co.uk
Book Design: Nicola Plumb
Picture Research: Frances Beard

ISBN: 978-1-62669-146-9

Printed and bound in China

10 9 8 7 6 5 4 3 2

CONTENTS

Fog in the Torres del Paine National Park, Patagonia, Chile

Carpathian Mountains,Ukraine.

EUROPE

ICELAND / NETHERLANDS / NORTHERN IRELAND / SPAIN / TURKEY / PORTUGAL / ITALY / GERMANY / FRANCE / ENGLAND / SLOVENIA / RUSSIA / SANTORINI / NORWAY / CROATIA / GREECE

VENICE

ITALY

Venice unabashedly calls itself La Serenissima- –'the Most Serene City'—and with good reason. An absolute mecca for the arts, the city possesses a long, illustrious history from the forging of a mercantile empire in the Adriatic and the Eastern Mediterranean to its role, along with Florence, at the epicenter of the Renaissance.

Part of the city's appeal is down to its fragility. In truth, Venice shouldn't still exist, since so much of the old city is perched above a 34 foot deep watery lagoon on ancient poles made mostly of alder wood. The city has survived centuries of political turmoil across Europe as well as flood tides, invasion by Napoleonic forces, two World Wars, and a continuing battle with the elements and its geography.

Venice is centered on an archipelago of 118 islands criss-crossed by more than 150 canals, which double as the old city's streets. Many of the islands are linked by the city's 400 bridges, amongst them the Rialto (until 1854 the only bridge across Venice's main artery, the Grand Canal), the Scalzi,and the infamous Bridge of Sighs. This connected the Doge's Palace – where Venice's ruler resided – to the *Prigioni Nuove* jail and was often the last view of the city seen by prisoners before their torture, incarceration, or death.

VENICE

GULF OF VENICE

BOLOGNA

SAN MARINO

A traditional gondola on the Grand Canal, Venice, Italy.

The city's mazy network of tiny back streets (one street, Calletta Varisco, is just 21 inches wide in places) and wider, cobbled thoroughfares and grand squares demand exploration as does its extensive network of canals and waterways, achieved via vaporetto water taxis or traditional gondola with their oar-wielding gondoliers. From a vantage point aboard one of these vessels, it is possible to spot the riot of architectural riches that built up over the centuries with Byzantine, Renaissance, Moorish, and Gothic architecture all present in great splendor.

The city has inspired wonder and plaudits for centuries; 16th century King of France, Henry III, is quoted as saying "If I were not King of France, I would choose to be a citizen of Venice" whilst famous American writer Henry James described it as "an orange gem resting on a blue glass plate" and Truman Capote likened it to "eating an entire box of chocolate liqueurs in one go." Such is its beauty that cities elsewhere – from Amiens and Bruges to Amsterdam and Trondheim – battle for second-place and the nickname 'the Venice of the North'.

Right: One of the many canals within the city which double as Venice's streets. Below left: Arcade of Doge's Palace. Below right: The Bridge of Sighs.

Right page: Doge's Palace on St. Mark's Square.

> " Venice, its temples and palaces did seem like fabrics of enchantment piled to heaven. "

Percy Bysshe Shelley, poet.

VATNAJÖKULL GLACIER CAVES

ICELAND

Europe's largest glacier by volume, Vatnajökull covers one twelfth of Iceland's land mass. Its ice has an average thickness of 1,300 feet and a maximum depth of over 3,300 feet. During the summer, an increase in temperatures causes meltwaters to form melting and forging crevasses, shafts, caves and caverns within the glacier. As winter comes, these ever-evolving caves harden and form stunning ice structures. Some, such as the Crystal Ice Cave that regularly occurs in the same place within this glacier, can hold 100 people with ease.

Only accessible during winter months – usually from November to late March and then only with a trained guide – these ever-evolving caves exhibit a range of textures and patterns with their ceilings often translucent enough to let light shine through them. Remarkable electric blue colors, billions of trapped air bubbles and lines of black sand and other debris caught up in the glacier's slow but unceasing movement make the textures and patterns unique yet temporary; the following season the cave will have changed or disappeared. Visitors sometimes experience a reminder of this giant river of ice's ongoing evolution with loud, sometimes unnerving, creaking or cracking noises caused by the glacier's gradual movement.

Ice cave in Vatnajökull glacier, Iceland.

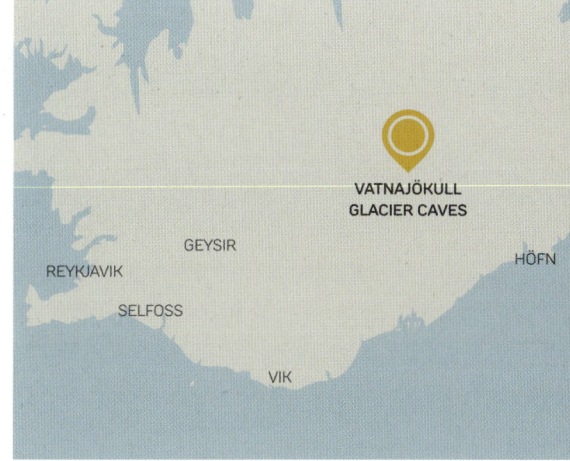

VATNAJÖKULL GLACIER CAVES

GEYSIR

REYKJAVIK

HÖFN

SELFOSS

VIK

KEUKENHOF GARDENS
NETHERLANDS

The Netherlands is synonymous with flowering spring bulbs such as daffodils and especially tulips. National Tulip Day is held in the country's largest city, Amsterdam, every third Saturday in January. It sees the city's large Dam Square turned into a giant temporary tulip garden with 200,000 flowers on show. Less than twenty miles west in the municipality of Lisse is a flower display commonly called the Garden of Europe. Seven million tulips, 35 times the amount found in Dam Square, are all planted by hand over an area covering an incredible 79 acres – equivalent to twice the area of New York's Grand Central Station.

Originally royal hunting grounds before they were turned into kitchen gardens to serve the neighboring castle, Keukenhof was transformed into a colorful demonstration of the Dutch bulb growers' art from 1950 onwards. The gardens vary; by turns, ornate and ornamental and natural and wild, with carpets of flowers blooming between glades of trees or along walkways and streams.

It's not just 800 varieties of tulips. Displays of other spring bulbs are prominent including daffodils, hyacinths, crocuses and narcissi, while pavilions and greenhouses contain orchids and other exotic plants. Whilst the grounds of Castle Keukenhof are open all year round, the Flower Gardens admit visitors from March to May with April peak viewing to see the flowers at the height of their colorful glory.

AMSTERDAM

KEUKENHOFF GARDENS

THE HAGUE

UTRECT

ROTTERDAM

16

This page: Peaceful miniature canals bisect the gardens, surrounded by a sublime array of spring color.
Left page, top: The formal gardens surrounding the Oranje Nassau pavilion.
Left page, bottom: Colorful waves of tulips within the gardens.

HALSTATT

AUSTRIA

Located between the Austrian cities of Salzburg and Graz and perched between the towering Dachstein mountains and the Hallstätter See Lake, this exquisitely scenic alpine settlement is one of the most photographed villages in Europe. Best reached by ferry across the lake, traces of human life extend back 7,000 years here and include some of the earliest salt mines in Europe, dating back around 2,500 to 2,800 years. The village and surrounding area became a UNESCO world heritage site in 1997.

Home to under 800 people, yet visited by a thousand times as many tourists each year, Hallstatt possesses charm in abundance from its small, cobbled market square to its wooden framed houses painted in pastel shades that reflect off the shimmering waters of the lake. Cars were recently banned from the village during the summer months to preserve its peace and charm. Such is the village's beauty that a Chinese corporation, Minmetals Land, cloned the village, building an accurate replica of its quaint houses and streets in the Chinese province of Guangdong in 2012 at a cost of over US$900 million.

KREMS

VIENNA

SALZBURG

ST. WOLFGANG

HALLSTATT

GRAZ

The snow covered village of Hallstatt in the Austrian Alps during winter time.

19

GIANT'S CAUSEWAY

NORTHERN IRELAND

A geological wonder and Northern Ireland's first UNESCO World Heritage site, the causeway consists of 40,000 hexagonal columns of basalt rock forming astonishing geometric patterns on the Antrim coast. According to Irish folklore, it was built by the mythical Irish giant, Fionn mac Cumhaill (also known as Finn McCool) as a bridge across the North Sea to the Scottish island of Staffa where he travelled to do battle with the Scottish giant Benandonner. The scientific fact may be less romantic but still stunning. The causeway was created some 60 million years ago when volcanic activity forced up molten basalt lava at a temperature of around 1,100°C through fissures in the Earth's surface only to be cooled rapidly by seawater. The resulting formations have excited and enticed humans for centuries.

As paintings and pamphlets about the basalt columns made them better known in the 18th and 19th centuries, so the numbers of visitors grew. In 1883, the world's first tram propelled by hydro-electric power began, carrying people from Portrush on a 8.7 mile route to the causeway. There, people encounter structures with such evocative names as the Giant's Chair, the Giant's Harp and Eyes, as well as the Organ, where the interlocking basalt columns form a passable impression of the pipes of a huge church organ. The Amphitheatre is a viewing point where varying lava flows and formations can be spied, not just the Causeway's world-famous columns.

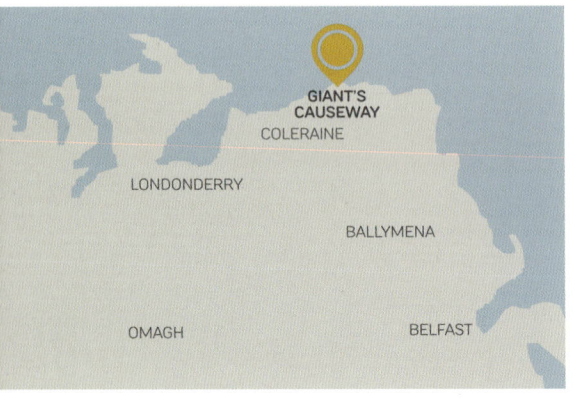

GIANT'S CAUSEWAY

COLERAINE

LONDONDERRY

BALLYMENA

OMAGH

BELFAST

The Giant's Causeway became a UNESCO World Heritage site in 1985 and remains free to visit and explore, often accompanied by the shrill cries of fulmars, petrels, and other seabirds that roost in the area.

Interior of Sagrada Familia with a view of the stained-glass windows, columns, and ceiling.

The intricate typographic carvings on the enormous wooden doors at the main entrance.

Exterior of Sagrada Familia.

SAGRADA FAMILIA

BARCELONA, SPAIN

Antoni Gaudí's great unfinished masterpiece bestrides the center of Barcelona, its existing towers viewable from many vantage points throughout the city. Although it polarizes opinion, few contest that the *Basílica de la Sagrada Família* - Basilica of the Holy Family - is undeniably striking and, to many eyes, outstandingly beautiful. When the original architect Francesc de Paula Villar resigned in 1883, just a year into the project's construction, 31 year old Gaudí took over. Instead of continuing with the relatively traditional gothic, three nave design, he masterminded a design transformation inspired by his own deep faith and the prevalence of geometric patterns in nature — from diatom-shaped windows to stone sculptures of fruit topping its spires. The natural symbolism extends inside with colorful columns supporting the vault branching out like trees and a staircase modelled on a snail's helicoidal spiral shell.

Only a small portion of the structure including one of its three sculptured facades was completed at his death, but work continued despite interruption during the Spanish Civil War (1936–39). The stated aim is to complete the basilica's total of 18 grand towers — twelve representing the apostles, four commemorating the evangelists, one representing the Virgin Mary, and the tallest representing Jesus Christ — by 2026, the centenary of Gaudí's death.

This picture and above: Religious stone figures detailed on the outside of the building.

PAMPLONA

SAGRADA FAMILIA
BARCELONA

ZARAGOZA

MADRID

TOLEDO   VALENCIA   PALMA
                                  DE MALLORCA

PAMUKKALE

TURKEY

This remarkable collection of cascading hot pools are fed by mineral-rich waters from 17 hot springs, ranging in temperature from 95 °F to 212 °F. Over thousands of years of deposition, calcium carbonate in the water hardens to form elaborate tiers of terraced ponds known as travertine structures. The multiple pools of milky-blue waters, surrounded by their bright white terraces with stalactite-like projections hanging down their edges, lend the location an ethereal, otherworldly air.

Located on the plain of Cürüksu near the town of Denizli in southwestern Turkey, Pamukkale's name comes from the Turkish for "cotton castle" or "cotton palace" from the slight resemblance to fields of cotton grown in central Turkey. Some sources state that the area was turned into a spa by the ancient Romans, but the reality is that it occurred earlier when the Attalid kings of Pergamon built baths, temples, and monuments here early in the 2nd century BCE. The town of Hierapolis built up above the pools, and was rebuilt several times before being abandoned by 1300 CE. Today, visitors can explore the ruins, enjoy the mineral-rich hot spring water channelled into artificial pools, and explore some of the natural pools barefoot.

AKHISAR

MANISA

IZMIR

NAZILLI

PAMUKKALE

AYDIN

DENIZLI

KUSADASI

BODRUM

MARMARIS

FETHIYE

Sunrise at the natural travertine pools and terraces, Pamukkale, Turkey.

BENAGIL SEA CAVE
PORTUGAL

Southern Portugal's rugged coastline is the result of the relentless pounding of the unceasing Atlantic Ocean waves. Hydraulic action and the erosive powers of wind and water have carved out a series of sea stacks, tiny bays with hidden beaches and coastal caves, none more astounding than just east of the small Algarve fishing and tourist village of Benagil which is home to one of southern Portugal's most celebrated beaches, Praia de Benagil.

The cave is only reachable by sea, although walkers can stand on top of its roof and peer in through the skylight-like hole in its ceiling, which illuminates the azure waters and the small beach found inside the cave's interior. Two graceful arches face the sea and together with the skylight in the cave's domed ceiling allow light to flood in. Hardier visitors, intent on being alone and at one with the cave, may head out at the crack of dawn in kayaks to reach this splendid monument to the power of ocean waves.

Benagil Sea Cave, Portugal.

LAKE BLED

CARNIOLAN REGION, SLOVENIA

Located 35 miles away from Slovenia's capital, Ljubljana, this enchanting lake in the Julian Alps has long been a haven for those seeking quiet, attractive vistas and crystal clear waters. The 6,960-foot-long, 97-foot-deep lake was formed during the last ice age after Bohinj Glacier melted and receded, and it has long been fabled to possess restorative powers. Scenic views from all angles abound from the rising slopes surrounding the waters, whilst on the north shore of the lake Bled Castle, with over 1,000 years of history, perches on a lofty, rocky precipice.

Traditional, flat-bottomed wooden boats called pletnas - crafted in a similar fashion to Italian gondolas - gently transport visitors from the lake shore to the only island in the whole of landlocked Slovenia, Blejski otok. There, one can climb 99 stone steps to reach the small 17th century church, dedicated to the Assumption of Mary, and ring the bell in its 117-foot-tall stone tower. According to the legend of the castle widow, Poliksena, the original bell fell into the lake during a storm.

JESENICE

BLED
LAKE BLED

RADOVIJICA

GORENJSKA

KRANJ

TOLMIN

ŠKOFJA LOKA

GORIŠKA

IDRIJA

A misty, autumnal view over Lake Bled and Slovenia's only island, Blejski otok.

ГРАЖДАНИНУ МИНИНУ И КНЯЗЮ ПОЖАРСКОМУ
БЛАГОДАРНАЯ РОССІЯ. ЛѢТА 1818

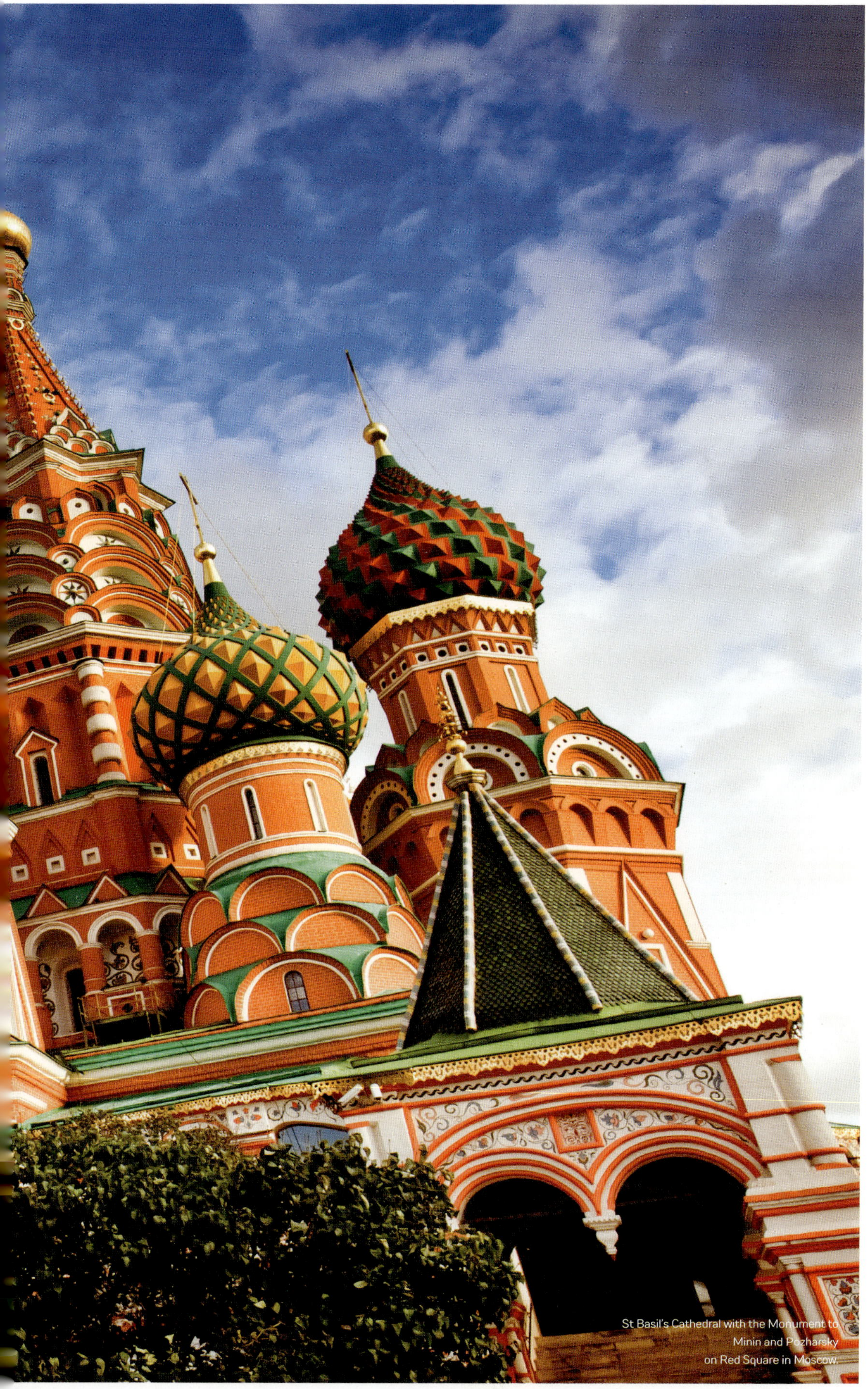

ST BASIL'S CATHEDRAL

MOSCOW, RUSSIA

Moscow's famed *Krasnaya Ploschad* or Red Square is a UNESCO World Heritage site. Located within its confines, close to the Kremlin, is a breath-taking cathedral that has no precedent in Russian architecture. Constructed on the orders of the infamous first Tsar of Russia, Ivan the Terrible, the Cathedral of the Intercession of the Most Holy Theotokos on the Moat is better known as St Basil's taking its name from a mystic from Yelokhovo who predicted a great fire that struck Moscow. Ivan the Terrible was said to be one of the pallbearers at his funeral and oversaw his canonization as a saint around 1580.

The building was originally a cluster of ten chapels with its arrangement of onion-shaped domes and spires said to represent the flickering flames of a fire. The domes were once gilded in tin but from the 1680s onwards, began to be painted, attaining their riot of bright colors mostly in the 18th century. Celebrating its 460th birthday in 2021, the architects of this magnificent structure, according to legend, were blinded on the orders of Ivan the Terrible so they would be unable to create anything so exquisitely beautiful again.

St Basil's Cathedral with the Monument to Minin and Pozharsky on Red Square in Moscow.

ST. PETERBURG
PSKOV
NOVGOROD
VOLOGDA
SMOLENSK
TVER'
YAROSLAVL'
KOSTROMA
ST BASIL'S CATHEDRAL
MOSCOW
KALUGA
IVANOVO
TULA
VLADIMIR
OREL
RYAZYN'

OIA

SANTORINI, GREECE

The volcanic island of Santorini is packed full of impressive viewing points and attractive villages. Oia is considered one of the most eye-catchingly beautiful. Small, homely houses line its streets in tiers up the steep coastal cliff. Some are quarried straight into the rock face whilst other, more ornate, *kapetanospita* or 'captain's houses' are found amongst its narrow thoroughfares. Many feature tiny front courtyards containing small *alitana* – flower beds full of fragrant jasmines, verbenas, honeysuckles and lavender. A 1956 earthquake severely damaged many structures in the village but repairs and reconstruction were made mindful of the local architecture and the village today has no unsightly electricity or phone lines above ground to spoil the stunning views.

More than seventy windmills were built on the island to harness the winds through the Cyclades to power grindstones to make flour. A windmill in Oia with its distinctive unclad wooden sail frames is a beacon for all budding photographers visiting the village, especially as sunset approaches. Oia is one of the most photographed locations in the entire Mediterranean. Lying below the main village and reached by 300 rocky steps is a small port called Ammoudi with small boats aplenty, willing to take tourists across to the neighboring island of Thirassia.

Sunset over Oia with Saint Spyridon and Anastasis Churches.

MILLAU VIADUCT
TARN VALLEY, FRANCE

A solution designed with a relatively prosaic purpose – to relieve congestion on the A75–A71 highway between Paris and southern France and Spain – yielded spectacular results in the form of this majestic viaduct. Spanning the Tarn valley, the four lane road deck, which weighs over 36,900 tons, stands a towering 890 feet above the river below, making it Europe's highest road bridge. Opened in December 2004, the 8,070 feet long, cable-stayed bridge took three years to build. It is supported by seven giant concrete piers, the tallest of which, at 1,125 feet high, stands 62 feet higher than France's Eiffel Tower.

Mere number crunching, however, doesn't do remote justice to the structure's delicate, slim grace and beauty. Designed by British architect Norman Foster to feel like one is flying a car across the valley, the bridge possesses astonishingly clean lines and a vulnerability as if something so slim could not possibly span two sets of tall hills and accept 15,000–20,000 motor vehicles thundering across its roads each day. Described by France-based reporter John Lichfield, as "too graceful to be real, like a row of giant storks standing on abnormally long, fragile legs," the bridge has helped slash journey times from as much as three hours to a mere 20 minutes.

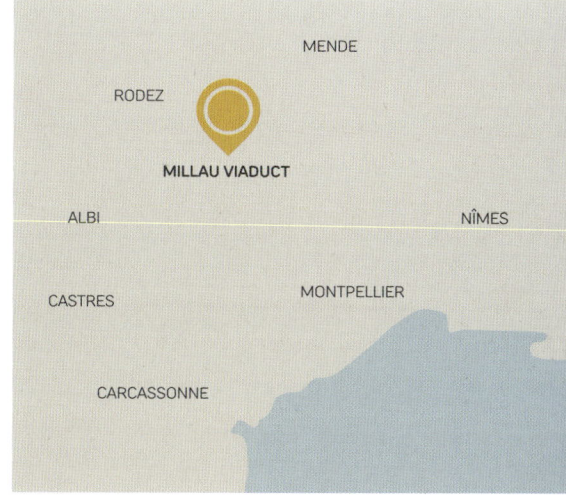

MENDE

RODEZ

MILLAU VIADUCT

ALBI   NÎMES

CASTRES   MONTPELLIER

CARCASSONNE

Millau Viaduct, France

AURORA BOREALIS

NEAR TROMSØ, NORWAY

These incredible flickering and changing light shows played out in the planet's upper atmosphere are the result of microscopic long-distance space travellers. Electrically-charged particles from the sun are propelled by the solar wind out into the solar system. Some of these particles complete a 93 million mile journey, heading into Earth's atmosphere where they collide and interact with gaseous particles such as oxygen and nitrogen, sometimes forming a spectacular specials effects circus in the night sky. No two nightly displays of these northern lights are the same and their unpredictability help give them an almost mystical allure.

Light-to-mid hues of green are the most common display, caused by collisions with oxygen molecules around 60 miles above earth, but yellows, blues, pinks and rare all-red lights, produced by high altitude oxygen at an altitude of 200 miles, all occur. Sensed with wonder since antiquity, they were named by Italian astronomer Galileo Galilei in 1619 from the ancient Roman goddess of the dawn, Aurora, and the Greek word for northern wind, *boreas*.

These 'northern lights' are potentially viewable in any extreme northerly location across the planet, free of light pollution from towns and cities. Fairbanks in Alaska, northern settlements in Canada such as Yellowknife and Whitehorse and Iceland are all popular vantage points. Many aurora hunters, however, travel to the Norwegian city of Tromsø then head out from there to more isolated locations, away from the city lights, to enjoy the show.

KVALØYSLETTA

TROMSØYA

HÅKØYA

TROMSØ

Aurora borealis over Tromsø.

The colorful Pena Palace.

Surrounding wall at the Castle of the Moors.

SINTRA
PORTUGAL

Found amongst the wooded hills of the Sintra Mountains, Sintra's cool climate and exotic gardens have lured royalty and aristocrats in summer for centuries. No less than six palaces are found around the municipality including the Town Palace in the city's colorful, historic center, Vila de Sintra. Narrow winding streets and pastel-colored villas greet visitors there, along with the clip-clopping sounds of numerous horse-drawn carriages for tourist tours.

Perched above the city on a hill, Pena Palace is a riot of color, all bright yellows and deep reds, as well as a mix of architectural influences. This former monastery was purchased by King consort Ferdinand in 1838 and transformed into a flamboyantly romantic castle, possessing both Islamic and medieval influences as well as many mythological statues, that would act as a summer retreat for the Portuguese royal family. On another hill lies a far older residence, the Castle of the Moors, built over 1,200 years ago.

Sintra's beauty has attracted legions of poets and writers including Hans Christian Andersen, who likened the palace's two cone-shaped chimneys to giant champagne bottles, and the romantic poet, Lord Byron, who exclaimed "Lo! Cintra's glorious Eden intervenes, in variegated maze of mount and glen."

Initiation Well at Quinta da Regaleira

TORRES VEDRAS

LOURES

SINTRA

AMADORA

LISBON

39

AMSTERDAM CANALS

NETHERLANDS

The Netherlands' largest city is a treasure trove of history from its ancient Dam Square and the world's oldest stock exchange to world-famous repositories of great artists such as Van Gogh and Rembrandt. It began as a 12th century fishing village and gained its name from the dam made across the River Amstel to prevent flooding. Deep channels dug for defence as moats and to manage the water in this flood-prone area changed function over the centuries to become *grachten* (canals). An explosion in canal building between 1585 and 1665 provided a city-wide transport network, now totalling 165 canals measuring almost 65 miles in length, and crossed by a staggering 1,281 bridges, according to Amsterdam's tourist authorities.

The canals and their bridges and walkways create a serene atmosphere to explore quite unlike the interior of any other city, aided by the profusion of bicycles and pedestrian-only thoroughfares. Lining many of its waterways, especially grand canals such as Prinsengracht, Herengracht, and Keizersgracht are beautiful old canal houses, narrow, crammed together and rising high with large gables. Many lean forward over the canals by design to enable heavy goods to be winched up from the waterways to the upper floors directly above. Most are ornately decorated - a legacy of the Dutch Golden Age of the 17th century and the region's rise as a major trading power.

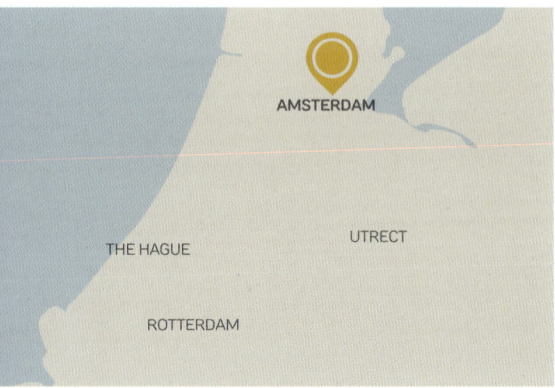

AMSTERDAM

THE HAGUE

UTRECT

ROTTERDAM

The Munttoren clock tower, as seen from the river Amstel at dusk

Crete Senesi, Tuscany, Italy.

Crete Senesi, Tuscany, Italy.

CRETE SENESI

TUSCANY, ITALY

Stretching along the valleys of the rivers Arbia, Asso and Ombrone, south-east of the beautiful Tuscan city of Siena, Crete Senesi possesses a gently undulating landscape of soft, rolling hills. Tell-tale rows of pine and cypress trees, some extraordinarily large and planted as simple wind breaks for farm fields, line winding roads and tracks whilst occasional farmhouses and even more sparingly, villages and small towns dot the region's landscape. Small woods of chestnut trees and fields of sunflowers sometimes contribute to subtle variations in this semi-arid region's rich coloration. It can all add up to a delight to the senses, especially if the region's famed white truffles and other local delicacies are also sampled and enjoyed.

Crete Senesi actually means Siennese clays — referring both to the greyish colored local soil called *mattaione* and the outcrops of badlands found in the region which bear a passing resemblance to a lunar landscape. During the Middle Ages, the area was known as the Desert of Accona for its otherworldly landscape. Picturesque medieval villages such as Buonconvento (meaning happy, lucky place in Latin), the quaint ancient town of Asciano and, 6 miles south, the Abbey of Monte Oliveto Maggiore are popular stopping points on a journey through the region.

FLORENCE
LIVORNO
CECINA
CRETE SENESI
PIOMBINO FOLLINICA
PORTOFERRAIO
GROSSETO
CAPOLIVERI

Crete Senesi, Tuscany, Italy.

COLOGNE CATHEDRAL

COLOGNE, GERMANY

The largest and most stunning example of gothic church architecture in Europe, the Kölner Dom or Cathedral Church of St Peter looms over Cologne and can be spied from almost every viewpoint in the city. Its first foundation stone was laid in 1248 but the cathedral wasn't completed for some 632 years. French troops occupied Cologne in the 1790s and used the unfinished church as a stable and hay barn. For a short time after its completion in 1880 until the construction of the Washington Monument in 1884, it was the tallest building in the world.

With a design based on France's Amiens Cathedral, Kölner Dom forms a Latin cross with two awe-inspiring towers. At 516 feet, 4 inches in height, the north tower is just two and three-quarter inches taller than the south. Anyone intrepid and fit enough to climb the 533 steps up the cathedral's south tower is rewarded with an astonishing view over the entire city. The tower's belfry holds the world's largest free-swinging church bell – a 52,000 lb behemoth of cast iron more than 10 feet in diameter and named St Petersglocke.

The cathedral and many of its treasures contained within survived 14 bombs dropped on it during World War II. Some of its incredible stained glass windows date back to the 13th century whilst the newest, installed in the south transept in 2007, uses more than 11,000 cubes in 72 different colors to cast a kaleidoscopic light effect onto the stone floors of the cathedral.

DUISBURG   ESSEN   DORTMUND

DÜSSELDORF

COLOGNE CATHEDRAL

AACHEN

SIEGEN

BONN

Cologne Cathedral at dusk.

Town dwellings in Göreme, Cappadocia

'Fairy chimneys' in Love Valley, Göreme, Cappadocia

CAPPADOCIA

TURKEY

It can be hard to believe that the fantastical formations here in Turkey's Central Anatolia region are not the work of a sci-fi movie set designer, but the result of geological processes. Erupting volcanoes blanketed the area many millions of years ago with a thick layer of ash which solidified into soft tuff rock later overlain by a layer of tougher and more robust basalt. Over the millennia, wind and water erosion has shaped these rocks into a strange alien landscape with swirling rock cones, pillars up to 130 feet in height, and 'fairy chimneys' with their bulbous bases and thin spires. Vistas are at their most surreal when the skies above are populated by dozens of bright hot air balloons intent on giving tourists an aerial panorama.

It hasn't just been natural forces shaping the land. Ancient peoples potentially as far back as the Hittite era (1200 BCE–1800 BCE) settled in the area and gouged caves as dwellings out of the soft rock. Rock-cut churches followed and some settlements expanded to form entire subterranean cities. Derinkuyu in southern Cappadocia descends over 200 feet below ground, contains numerous levels and ventilation shafts, and is believed capable of holding a population of up to 20,000 with living quarters, workshops, storerooms and places of worship.

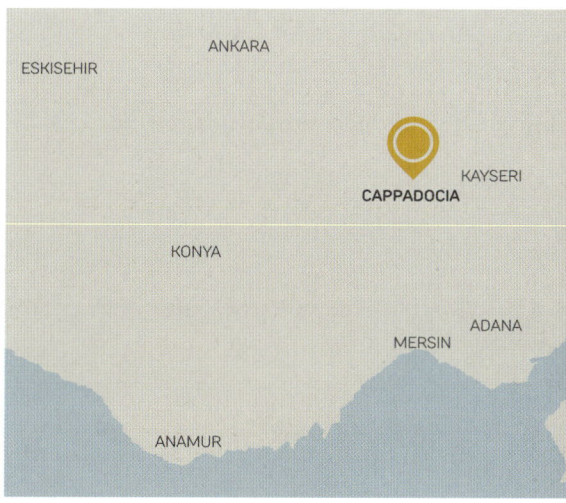

Ancient ruins of cave dwellings in Göreme, Cappadocia.

NEUSCHWANSTEIN CASTLE

BAVARIA, GERMANY

On becoming King of Bavaria as a teenager, Ludwig II decided to squander much of his personal royal fortune on a fairy-tale castle overlooking Schwansee (Swan Lake) in southern Germany. It was meant as a tribute to Richard Wagner, who Ludwig admired enormously, dedicating many of the rooms inside to the classical composer.

Work began violently in 1869 with the top 26 feet of the hill blown away by explosives and 17 years later, when the king died, only 14 of its planned 200 or more rooms were completed. Ludwig contented himself with living in the gatehouse, completed in 1872. Although harking back to the romantic ideal of a Germanic knight's castle from the Middle Ages, Neuschwanstein was built using the latest technology of the time including steam-powered cranes. It was also equipped lavishly inside with innovative forced air central heating, automatic flushing toilets (unheard of at the time), and two new-fangled telephones even though there was no one for the king to call.

Inside its white limestone clad towers and walls was the main building, the Palas. This had five floors including the 89 feet by 33 feet Hall of Singers where Ludwig planned to stage and enjoy operatic performances. Next to his study on the fourth floor of the Palas was an indoor artificial waterfall. Now visited by over 1.3 million tourists each year, the castle was an inspiration for Walt Disney's Cinderella castle in the movie of the same name.

ULM
AUGSBURG
MUNICH
MEMMINGEM
GARMISCH-PARTENKIRCEN
NEUSCHWANSTEIN CASTLE

Neuschwanstein Castle, Germany.

GEIRANGERFJORD
NORWAY

Sculpted by glaciers, fjords are long, narrow inlets surrounded by steep-sided land or cliffs on three sides with the fourth side usually open to the sea. These epic constructions are found along a number of nation's coastlines including New Zealand and Chile, but they are most synonymous with Norway and Geirangerfjord is one of that country's most spectacular examples. Wild, rugged and outstandingly beautiful, the fjord spans a length of 9.3 miles and is almost a mile wide in places. Its clear, cold waters extend more than 800 feet down whilst looming over the fjord are sharp-edged mountains 6,000 feet or more above the water's surface.

Striking cliffs, tree-lined lower slopes and a number of scenic waterfalls greet those fortunate enough to venture along the fjord. The Suitor and Seven Sisters Falls lie on opposite cliffs facing each other as if one is trying to woo the other whilst water cascades delicately over the Brudesløret or Bridal Veil waterfall.

At the head of the fjord lies its only major settlement, the small village of Geiranger, whose 250–strong population is overwhelmed by the tens of thousands of visitors, most disgorged from the more than 140 cruise ships who travel up the fjord and dock using the village's small port. Some travellers head from here along the Trollstigen or Trolls Road's dramatically snaking route with its eleven hairpin turns which makes for one of Europe's most exhilarating road trips.

Geirangerfjord, Norway.

TRONDHEIM

MOLDE

INFJORDEN

VALLDALEN   BJORLI

GEIRANGERFJORD   LESJAVERK

BISMO

CINQUE TERRE

LIGURIA, ITALY

Remote and perfectly preserved, these five small, almost unbearably charming fishing villages are found on Italy's northwestern coast, west of La Spezia. Collectively named the Cinque Terre meaning "Five Earths", the five villages: Corniglia, Manarola, Riomaggiore, Vernazza and, the largest, Monterosso al Mare, all perch precariously on the rugged coastline at the eastern end of the Italian Riviera. Founded over 600 years ago and only accessible by foot for centuries, they each look like they have grown organically out of the surrounding rock.

There's a timeless appeal to the villages' sharply winding streets and their many tiers of brightly painted houses festooned with flower boxes and wooden window shutters, but each village has its own distinct appeal and attractions – from Monterosso's beaches and Vernazza's *caruggi* (steep, narrow lanes) and picturesque natural harbor to Manorola's tiny piazza and its 14th century Church of San Lorenzo. Manarola and neighboring Riomaggiore are connected by the Via dell'Amore (Lover's Lane), a winding footpath carved into the rocks and overhanging the sea. Only the village of Corniglia, with its location on a 300-foot-tall promontory and surrounded on three sides by vineyards and terraces, lacks direct access to the sea.

Vernazza in Cinque Terre, Liguria, Italy.

Manarola Village, Cinque Terre, Liguria, Italy.

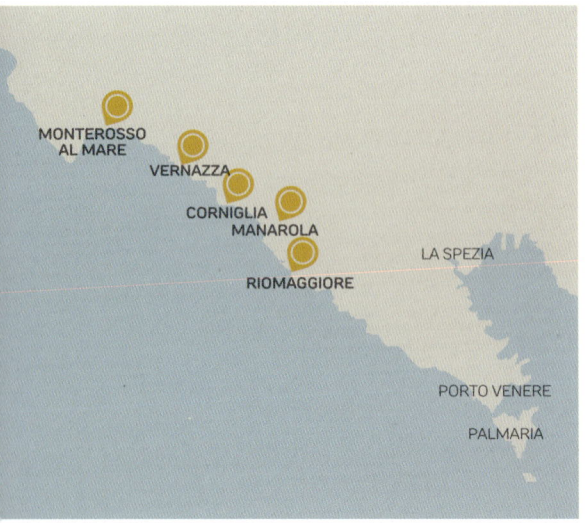

MONTEROSSO AL MARE

VERNAZZA

CORNIGLIA
MANAROLA

LA SPEZIA

RIOMAGGIORE

PORTO VENERE

PALMARIA

Port of Vernazza, Cinque Terre, Liguria, Italy.

Durdle Door is a natural limestone arch on the Jurassic Coast, Dorset

JURASSIC COAST

ENGLAND

This 96-mile stretch of supremely pretty southern English coastline is a genuine slice of geological history and one of the first places to give people insight into the prehistoric world. Stretching from Old Harry Rocks near Swanage in Dorset to Orcombe Point in Devon, this series of coastal cliffs facing the English Channel comprises 185 million years of history, spanning Triassic, Jurassic and Cretaceous periods. A Dorset-born woman, Mary Anning, became the first great fossil hunter in the early 19th century along this coast, discovering ammonites, plesiosaurs, ichthyosaurs and pterosaur fossils in and around her native Lyme Regis. Thousands more continue to be uncovered in other fossil hotspots along the coast including Charmouth, Chippel Bay, and Watton Cliff.

Erosion over time has created some simply sublime structures from the tight, horseshoe-shaped bay of Lulworth Cove to splendid sea arches such as Durdle Door and Chesil Bank - an 18-mile-long barrier beach. Sharp cliffs, some stained red or pink by iron oxide streaks, mix with charming coves and sandy or pebble beaches. Walks along stretches of this coast additionally offer atmospheric coastal villages and swathes of unspoilt rolling downs and other traditional southern English countryside.

Corfe Castle, Dorset.

Ammonite fossil at Lyme Regis, Dorset.

Lulworth Cove, Dorset.

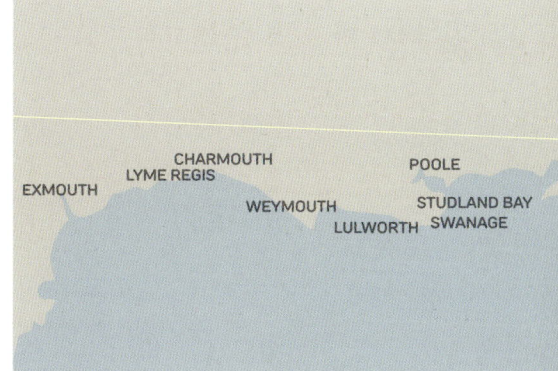

EXMOUTH
CHARMOUTH
LYME REGIS
WEYMOUTH
LULWORTH
POOLE
STUDLAND BAY
SWANAGE

THE ALHAMBRA
GRANADA, SPAIN

A triumph of Moorish architecture and art, this fortress and palace was built on al-Sabika Hill in the 13th and 14th centuries and overlooks the beautiful Spanish city of Granada. Taking its name from the Arabic for "the red fort," the Alhambra's stunning rooms are frequently decorated with stained glass and stucco – plaster carved with intricate designs – and richly augmented with paintings on stretched leather, incredibly detailed mosaics made of thousands of tiles in geometric patterns and other outstanding examples of Arabic art.

From its stout-walled fortress, the Alcazaba, to the contrasting Charles V palace, crammed into the grounds and built later, there is much to enjoy here. The Alhambra's airy courtyards open out onto a series of tranquil gardens and ponds, pools, and fountains all fed by a series of channels and aqueducts from the river Darro some five miles away. The fountain with its 12 lion statues in the Patio de los Leones (Court of the Lions) is one of the Alhambra's most photographed sights.

Separated from the Alhambra by a ravine is the Generalife, (from the Arabic Jannat al-'Arif meaning Garden of the Architect). This summer palace with its pavilions, courtyards, and scenic gardens was built between 1302 and 1309 and reached by a covered walkway suspended over the ravine.

The Alhambra, Granada, Spain.

SEVILLE

THE ALHAMBRA
GRANADA

MALAGA   MOTRIL   ALMERIA
                    ROQUETAS
                    DE MAR
MARBELLA

GIBRALTAR

Intricate, carved walls within The Alhambra.

Decorated pillars and arches along the famous Court of the Lions, Alhambra.

Nasrid Palaces within The Alhambra.

The medieval town of Rothenburg ob der Tauber.

ROTHENBURG OB DER TAUBER

GERMANY

A clutch of German medieval cities and settlements have largely escaped the ravages of time, amongst them Miltenberg, Bamberg, and Michelstadt. Rothenburg, perched on the banks of the River Tauber, is considered Germany's best-preserved town of all. Ringed within one and a half miles of 14th-century fortress walls, Rothenburg's *Altstadt* or old town looks like a classic fairy tale retelling with its cobbled streets, tottering and crooked half-timbered, pastel-colored medieval dwellings, Gothic churches, and the delightful triangular Plönlein square, all beautifully preserved and best viewed under lamplight or as the sun sets.

In the 15th century, when the town's St. Jakob's Church was finally completed, Rothenburg ob der Tauber reached its peak of power and prosperity, when it far exceeded the populations resident in either Frankfurt or Munich. Today, it is promoted as a major tourist destination situated on the Romantic Road. This route through Bavaria and Baden-Württemberg was a key trade route centuries ago, but is now known for its rich concentration of historic and scenic landmarks including towns such as Nördlingen and Dinkelsbühl and fairy-tale castles like Neuschwanstein.

Left page: The historic town of Rothenburg ob der Tauber, Franconia, Bavaria, Germany.

Medieval city wall in the old town of Rothenburg ob der Tauber.

SELJALANDSFOSS WATERFALL

ICELAND

Scenic Seljalandsfoss is a 190-feet-tall waterfall, fed by waters from the river Seljalandsá as it it flows towards the sea. The river itself can trace its source back to the Eyjafjallajökull glacier. The volcano beneath this glacier was a major news story in 2010 when its eruption showered Europe with volcanic dust clouds and provoked havoc with multiple airport closures.

Fortunately, a visit to this beautiful waterfall is more tranquil, an experience enhanced by the soaking one receives from the perpetual fine mist cast by the falling waters. Iceland boasts large numbers of waterfalls, but what makes Seljalandsfoss unique is the path that takes hikers behind the falls into a small cave, from where it is possible to look out through the cascading waters at southern Iceland's bleak yet beautiful coastal approaches. Close by and to the north of Seljalandsfoss is the neglected but almost equally attractive Gljúfrabúi waterfall, which, partially obscured behind a rock face and with a name meaning "dweller of the gorge," is something of a genuinely hidden gem.

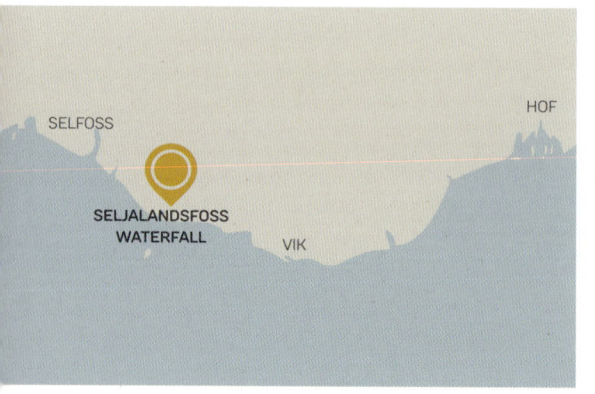

SELFOSS

HOF

SELJALANDSFOSS WATERFALL

VIK

Seljalandsfoss waterfall.

TOWER BRIDGE
LONDON, ENGLAND

As Victorian London boomed and its population grew, so did the traffic on its lands and along the River Thames. A new bridge was needed to the eastern side of the city but one that didn't disrupt the steady flow of shipping. The City of London Corporation launched a competition and received more than 50 entrants. The winning design by John Woolfe Barry and Horace Jones combined suspension bridge features with a bascule design (from the French for see-saw). Since its opening in 1894, it has become a London icon and one of the city's most recognizable and attractive landmarks.

The 800-foot-long bridge required 31 million bricks along with 70,000 tons of concrete and 11,000 tons of steel during its construction. Its ornate twin towers, both 213 feet tall and exhibiting Victorian gothic architectural flourishes, support a hinged central section split into two parts. This was raised by immense steam engines powering a hydraulic lift system, replaced in the 1970s by an electro-hydraulic system. Thousands of people cross the bridge today, some enjoying the stunning views of London from its high walkway, parts of which are floored in transparent plexiglass for visitors to look down as well as out and across the city.

Tower Bridge, London

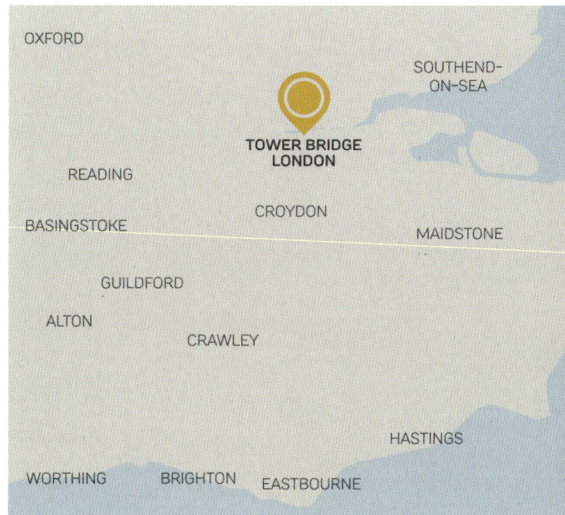

OXFORD

SOUTHEND-ON-SEA

TOWER BRIDGE
LONDON

READING

CROYDON

BASINGSTOKE

MAIDSTONE

GUILDFORD

ALTON

CRAWLEY

HASTINGS

WORTHING   BRIGHTON   EASTBOURNE

COLOSSEUM
ROME, ITALY

A merciless monument to the ancient Romans, their engineering prowess and desire for bloodthirsty entertainment, the Colosseum or *Amphitheatrum Flavium* was constructed on the orders of Emperor Vespasian around 72 CE. It was completed by his son and successor, Titus, eight years later and opened with a 100 day orgy of brutality and killing. Amongst the entertainments were gladiatorial contests, public executions, and wild animal fights, some featuring rhinoceros, elephants, and lions. As many as 9,000 beasts were put to the sword during these inaugural games, according to the ancient Roman historian Suetonius.

It would not be the end of the bloodshed as the Colosseum stayed in use for nigh on four centuries. Crowds numbering more than 50,000 entered its 80 entrances and crammed into the 620-foot-long, 513-foot-wide freestanding amphitheatre, the biggest in the Roman world. They came to witness gladiatorial bouts between trained ex-soldiers, criminals, or slaves, armed in differing ways, all trained at gladiator schools before, on occasion, battling to the death. The largest of Rome's gladiator training centers, the *Ludus Magnus*, was rediscovered in 1937 close to the Colosseum and linked to the arena by an underground tunnel. The Colosseum also contained vaults below ground where wild animals were held in cages and winched into the arena for battle. Today, after almost two millennia of fire and earthquake damage as well as the looting of its sparkling outer covering of polished travertine stone, the multiple banks of arches of the Colosseum still retain their sense of the spectacular.

Sunrise at The Colosseum, Rome

LAKE KÖNIGSSEE

BAVARIA, GERMANY

One forty-fifth of Germany's total area is covered in water, most of it in the form of the country's thousands of lakes. Königssee is arguably its most stunning. Situated in Bavaria within the Berchtesgaden Alps, this five-mile-long stretch of water feels a lot like a fjord, formed by glacial action and surrounded on all sides by imposing and towering mountains that produce a booming echo.

With petrol-engined boats banned from its crystal clear waters since 1909, only rowing boats and electric vessels glide silently and serenely across the surface, carrying people to locations such as the isolated church of Sankt Bartholomä, only reachable by boat or an arduous mountain hiking trail.

The lake shore rises by turns shallowly, then steeply with its wooded fringes blossoming in spring with violets and cowslips as well as providing habitats for foxes, chamois, red and roe deer, and ibex. Although humming with tourists in the high season, the lake shores are not overly developed in places, allowing visitors to commune with nature and the impressive post-glacial landscape. In the words of Florian Hallinger, captain of one of Königsee's electric boats, "You can still enjoy nature here: it is pure and modest without a hint of kitsch."

LANDSHUT

AUGSBURG

MUNICH

STARNBERG

ROSENHEIM

LAKE KÖNIGSSEE

Lake Königssee, Germany.

PLITVICE LAKES NATIONAL PARK
CROATIA

Croatia's gem was designated one of Europe's first UNESCO World Heritage sites in 1979 in recognition of the unique beauty of its limestone landscape and crystalline lakes. These terraced lakes, 16 in total, tumble into each other via a series of eye-catchingly exquisite cascades and waterfalls. When viewed from one of a number of wooden bridges or walkways overhead, they exude a mystical, almost magical air. Surrounding the lakes is attractive, rugged countryside populated by large numbers of beech, fir, and spruce trees and home to more than 350 species of butterflies and 150 species of birds.

The lakes are divided into twelve upper and four lower lakes, all fed by mineral-rich waters from both small rivers above ground and subterranean water sources. The barriers between each pool of water are the result of years of interaction between the calcium carbonate rich waters and bacteria, algae, and mosses. To preserve its delicate travertine barrier structures, swimming is forbidden in the lakes. At the end of the lower lakes, the water makes its longest drop over Croatia's highest waterfall, Veliki Slap. A popular location for wedding ceremonies, the water tumbles down here 256 feet into the river Korana below.

Plitvice Lakes National Park, Croatia.

Plitvice Lakes National Park, Croatia.

Waterfalls at Plitvice Lakes National Park, Croatia.

METEORA MONASTERIES
THESSALY, GREECE

Perched precipitously on the pinnacles of rocky columns in the Plain of Thessaly, this extraordinary collection of religious buildings redefines the phrase "top of the world." People have called caves their homes in this region of Central Greece for millennia but around 700 years ago, Christian hermits and monks began living on top of the sandstone pillars, some of which are 60 million years old. Separating themselves from the world, the buildings they constructed began as simple living quarters but developed into fully-blown monasteries 'suspended in the air' — the meaning of the word, *meteora*.

Around 24 of these extraordinary monuments were constructed, some of which have been lost to earthquake damage or ruined by wars including bombing during World War II. Astonishingly, six fully function as active monasteries to this day; the largest, the Great Meteoron, sits atop Platýs Líthos or Broad Rock over 1900 feet above sea level. Since 1961, the 16th century Monastery of Rousanou has been a convent for a small group of nuns.

The monasteries remained isolated from the outside world for centuries. Many used winches to lift supplies up the rocky columns whilst the Monastery of Varlaam received a stone staircase to its top in 1923, over 400 years after the building was constructed. In more recent times a funicular train connects Agia Triada Monastery with the outside world as does an iron and wooden bridge for Rousanou Monastery.

A majestic view of the monasteries on the Greek Meteora rocks.

ULLSWATER
LAKE DISTRICT, ENGLAND

The second largest of northwest England's lakes behind Windermere, Ullswater has a powerful yet serene beauty that attracts many visitors seeking a break from the busier visitor attractions of the English Lake District.

A typical ribbon lake formed by glacier action after the last Ice Age, the lake measures 7.3 miles long and 0.63 miles at its widest point. Its still, dark waters are surrounded by rocky shorelines broken with many small coves and beaches and clumps of forest where the tree trunks are blanketed by the rich vibrant greens of lichens and mosses. Swathes of flowering bulbs greet visitors in springtime, for this was the place where English Romantic poet William Wordworth obtained inspiration for his famous 1804 poem, 'Daffodils'. Of Ullswater itself, Wordsworth wrote, "It is the happiest combination of beauty and grandeur which any of the lakes affords."

Donald Campbell set a world water speed record on the lake in 1955, thundering across its surface at a speed of 202.32 mph in the jet engine-powered *Bluebird K7* hydroplane. Today's vessels offer far more genteel and quiet voyaging. The lake is a haven for dinghy sailing and is served by quaint, traditional steamers which link lakeside destinations including Pooley Bridge, Howtown, Aira Force, and Ullswater's largest settlement, Glenridding, from where many hardy souls set off to tackle Helvellyn, England's third highest mountain.

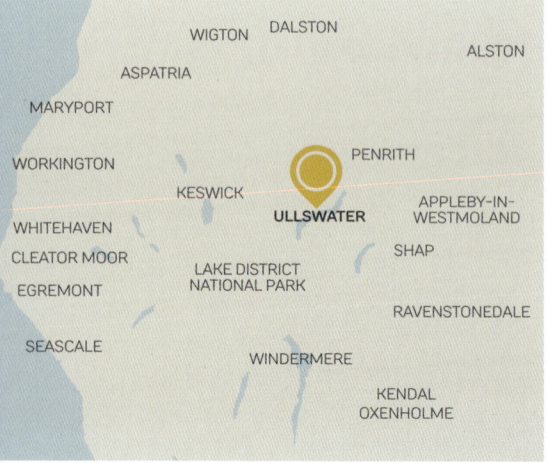

A view of Ullswater from Arnison Crag

REINE

LOFOTEN ISLANDS, NORWAY

Deep inside the Arctic Circle lies Norway's most picturesque village. It is located on the eastern side of the island of Moskenesøya, one of the southernmost Lofoten islands, an archipelago in the Norwegian Sea. This tiny village is home to fewer than 350 hardy souls who mostly make their living from trawling the fish-rich local waters and drying their resulting catch in the biting cold air to create the popular Nordic delicacy of stockfish.

The villagers are vastly outnumbered in the summer months both by gulls and other seabirds, whose shrill cries are a constant accompaniment, and by tourists who flock to see its spectacular location for themselves. Few are disappointed by the congruence of wooden rorbu – Norwegian stilt houses, most painted a deep red – bounded by the deep waters of the surrounding Reinefjord with snow-capped mountains in the distance. Towering over the village are the sharp granite features of Reinebringen – a rocky outcrop 1,470 feet high. Climbing to the top, aided by 820 stone steps, affords magnificent views across much of southern Moskenesøya and the neighboring villages of Sakrisøy and Hamnøy.

Lofoten islands, Norway.

VESTVÅGØY

LEKNES · STAMSUND

GRAVDAL

RAMBERG · SENNESVIK

BALLSTAD

FLAKSTADØYA

NUSFJORD

KIRKEFJORD

MOSKENESØYA

REINE

PALACE OF VERSAILLES

FRANCE

Surveying the extravagant pomp and grandeur of one of the world's most famous palaces, it is hard to believe that it began life as a humble hunting lodge built by French king Louis XIII in 1623. His son, Louis XIV, seeking a move out of Paris, ordered the construction there of an unrestrained and unbounded monument to his own perceived greatness. The result, involving 36,000 workers building a palace of 700 rooms 12 miles southwest of Paris, almost bankrupted France. Subsequent monarchs added and improved on the original design up until the French Revolution in 1789. Louis XV, for example, commissioned the building of the ornate Royal Opera, a large theatre inside Versailles seating 1,200 and lit by 10,000 candles.

Versailles is a study in extreme opulence drawn on an incredibly grand scale. The palace's stables, for example, were so large they could hold up to 12,000 horses, the kitchens were staffed by 500 workers, whilst its mighty gardens, formed largely from drained swampland, housed an extraordinary 1,400 fountains (607 of which survive to this day) as well as 400 original sculptures. Louis XIV even insisted on his own mile-long, 203–foot-wide Grand Canal within the grounds.

Louis moved his court to Versailles by 1682 and effectively governed France from this grand palace, having a second, smaller palace, Le Grand Trianon, built within its grounds. The wealthiest and most powerful members of European society craved an

NANTERRE
RUEIL-MALMAISON
NEUILLY-SUR-SEINE
LA CELLE-SAINT-CLOUD
PARIS
BOULOGNE-BILLANCOURT
LE CHESNAY
ISSY-LES-MOULINEAUX
PALACE OF VERSAILLES
CLAMART

Magnificent Marble Court (*Cour de Marbre*) within Palace of Versailles.

" Versailles! It is wonderfully beautiful! You gaze and stare and try to understand that it is real, that it is on the earth, that it is not the Garden of Eden—but your brain grows giddy, stupefied by the world of beauty around you, and you half believe you are the dupe of an exquisite dream. "

Mark Twain, in The Innocents Abroad (1869).

invitation and jostled for primacy in his presence as they observed *le Roi Soleil* (the Sun King, for the way his entire court and, indeed, France orbited around him like planets do a star) living a life of enormous pomp and ceremony.

With a popularity outstripping another French icon, the Eiffel Tower, tourist numbers today approach eight million a year. They come for a trip back in time to an era of absolute monarchy and a glimpse of the vast riches it entailed, from the gold leaf covered entrance gates to the truly extraordinary *Galerie des Glaces* (Hall of Mirrors). At a time when mirrors were almost as precious as diamonds, a household could signify their wealth by owning one small mirror. This huge hall, 239.5 feet long and 40 feet high, was lined with 357 large mirrors and lit by in excess of 3,000 candles creating a blazing corridor of light. This hall was where the Treaty of Versailles was signed in 1919 in the aftermath of World War I.

Palace of Versailles.

Royal chapel, Palace of Versailles.

Ceiling paintings, Palace of Versailles.

Ceiling paintings, Palace of Versailles.

The formal gardens, Palace of Versailles.

Hand Sculpture, the symbol of Atacama Desert in Chile.

CENTRAL AND SOUTH AMERICA

PERU / BRAZIL / GALAPAGOS ISLANDS / ARGENTINA / BOLIVIA / CHILE / COSTA RICA / BELIZE / GUATEMALA / MEXICO / EASTER ISLAND

MACHU PICCHU
CENTRAL ANDES, PERU

In 1911, American explorer Hiram Bingham made a sensational discovery whilst on the hunt for the fabled lost city of Vilcabamba – the legendary last refuge of the Inca emperor as they retreated from the invading Spaniards. Perched on top of a steep, narrow saddle of land between two mountains and lying abandoned for four centuries was a lost city of the Incas. Built around 1460 CE, Machu Picchu had been left unscathed by invading Spanish conquistadors and untouched by tomb robbers or treasure hunters. It remains one of the single most spectacular archaeological finds ever made.

Surrounded by thick jungle and often shrouded in low clouds which augment its mystery and wonder, Machu Picchu was built with astonishing precision and craft. Its 200 buildings and elegant plazas connected by more than 100 stairways across its many levels all flow together with consummate skill. Astonishingly, the Incas did not use cement, iron or steel tools, have pack animals like oxen or horses to call upon nor used the wheel. Yet, they managed to fashion an extraordinary and beautiful settlement, partly built out of giant granite blocks, some weighing in excess of 40 tons, yet all fitted together without mortar or cement so perfectly that it is impossible to slip a blade of grass between the joints.

PUCALLPA

CHIMBOTE

HUÁNUCO

LIMA

MACHU PICCHU

CUSCO

ICA

PUNO

AREQUIPA

The taller Huayna Picchu mountain looms over Machu Picchu in the distance

" Few romances can ever surpass that of the granite citadel on top of the beetling precipices of Machu Picchu, the crown of Inca Land. "

Hiram Bingham.

Machu Picchu is separated into residential and workplace areas as well as palaces, large, open plazas, and temples. These include the Temple of the Three Windows and the one circular building in the city, the Temple of the Sun, whose windows are positioned astronomically to catch the first rays of the summer and winter solstice. Step terraces cut into the steep, sheer hillsides provided narrow strips of land to grow maize, quinoa, and other crops for its 750 inhabitants.

Visitors who take the steep bus ride from the small town of Agua Calientes 2,000 feet below or make the strenuous 90 minute walk up the winding mountain road are rewarded with extraordinary views in all directions. One of the very best is from the building dubbed the Guardhouse at the break of day with the sun's rays steadily illuminating Machu Picchu's many tiers and structures. As Ruth M. Wright states in *The Machu Picchu Guidebook: A Self-Guided Tour*, "It is a breathtaking, almost spiritual experience, and one you will never forget."

The corners of this sculpted Intihuatana stone known as 'the hitching post of the sun' orientate towards the four major compass points. The stone was used as a solar calendar.

The precipitous nature of Machu Picchu's location, 50 miles northwest of Cusco, can be seen in this photo. With its farming terraces and natural springs, archaeologists believe the settlement was self-sufficient and not reliant on the surrounding lands of Peru.

Steeply cut terraces denote the agricultural sector of Machu Picchu. Far below the fast-flowing Urubamba river runs. A rope bridge over the river provided the Incas with a secret entrance to the city.

SUGAR LOAF MOUNTAIN

RIO DE JANEIRO, BRAZIL

An icon of Brazil, Pão de Açúcar or Sugarloaf Mountain rises sharply upwards from the peninsula that juts out of Guanabara Bay in the booming Brazilian city of Rio de Janeiro. Many of the more than 1.5 million foreign tourists who visit the city each year take a trip up the mountain to experience stunning views of Rio and Guanabara Bay, which forms a large natural harbor below. The mountain is believed to be 600 million years old and formed from tough granite and quartz which has resisted erosion far more than the surrounding rocks. It stands 396m high.

The local Tamoios native South Americans called the mountain Pau-nh-açuquã, meaning "tall, pointy hill on its own," but Sugarloaf got its current name from Portuguese settlers and traders in the 16th and 17th centuries. At the time, sugar was extracted from cane as a liquid and poured into rounded cone-shaped moulds before being carried away by ships. The moulds looked much like the mountain hence its name. Some of the more athletic visitors choose the hard way up the mountain, climbing its sheer walls or scrambling up steep tracks and steps on foot. Others take the leisurely scenic route via cable cars, which first ran in 1912 and involves a change of car at the neighboring hill, Morro da Urca.

GLÓRIA
RIO COMPRIDO
LARANJEIRAS
FLAMENGO
BOTAFOGO   SUGAR LOAF MOUNTAIN
HUMAITÁ
LAGOA
COPACABANA
IPANEMA

Sugar Loaf Mountain, Rio De Janeiro, Brazil.

GALÁPAGOS ISLANDS
PACIFIC OCEAN

By turns bleak and beautiful, the Galápagos is made up of 19 islands and over 100 far smaller islets or rocky outcrops in the Pacific Ocean. The archipelago sits over a volcanic hotspot and at the confluence of differing ocean currents, helping to give the islands a milder climate than many locations perched on the Equator. In stunning isolation, more than 500 miles from the South American coast, life evolved differently here to elsewhere. Famed British naturalist Charles Darwin, who developed his theory of evolution after visiting the islands in 1835 aboard HMS *Beagle*, described them as "a little world within itself."

This has given the islands an unparalleled concentration of endemic species. Approximately 80 percent of the land birds, 97 percent of its reptiles and land mammals, and over 30 percent of its plant species are found here and nowhere else. These include the iconic 550 pound giant Galápagos tortoise, the world's only flightless cormorants, and the Galápagos penguin — the only penguin species found in the northern hemisphere.

Stunning lava formations mix with unusual cacti and prickly pear trees, scrub bush, and sudden flecks of brightly-colored creatures, none more so than the technicolor Sally Lightfoot crabs who are often found picking nits off the backs of marine iguanas before the iguanas defy their stereotype as land dwellers by plunging into the Pacific – making them the only ocean-going lizard.

PINTA

GENOVESA

MARCHENA

SANTIAGO

NORTH SEYMOUR & MOSQUERA

FERNANDINA   RABIDA   BALTRA

PINZÓN   SANTA CRUZ

ISABELA   SANTA FÉ   SAN CRISTÓBAL

TORTUGA

FLOREANA

GARDNER   ESPAÑOLA

Marine iguana (Amblyrhynchus cristatus) on Santa Cruz Island, Galápagos Islands.

A family of Galápagos tortoises

View of two beaches on Bartolomé Island in the Galápagos Islands.

IGUAZÚ FALLS
ARGENTINA / BRAZIL

Iguazú means "Big Water" in the local Guarani language but this is somewhat of an understatement. When she first set sight on the falls that define part of Brazil's border with Argentina, first lady Eleanor Roosevelt is reported to have exclaimed "Poor Niagara!" Iguazú is monumentally huge — twice as high and almost three times wider than those on the US-Canadian border. Visitors often head for the largest curtain of water produced by these falls - the atmospherically-named *La Garganta del Diablo* or the Devil's Throat.

It consists of 275 separate drops, ranging in height from 196 to 270 feet, which together stretch an incredible distance of 1.7 miles. During the rainy season that extends from November to March, the rate of water flowing over the falls may reach 450,000 cubic feet — the equivalent of filling 300 Olympic-sized swimming pools every minute. National parks were established in both Argentina (in 1934) and Brazil, five years later, to conserve the rich biodiversity of the subtropical area surrounding the falls, which include 2,000 species of plants, 80 different mammals, including jaguars, and more than 400 species of birds.

Iguazú Falls, Argentina / Brazil.

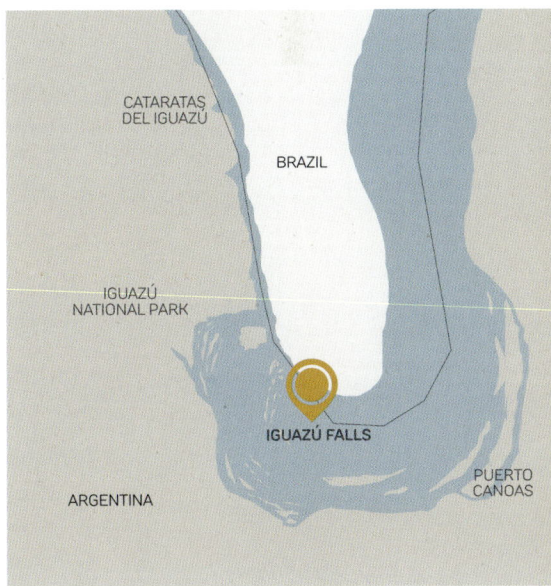

CATARATAS DEL IGUAZÚ

BRAZIL

IGUAZÚ NATIONAL PARK

IGUAZÚ FALLS

ARGENTINA

PUERTO CANOAS

SALAR DE UYUNI

ALTIPLANO, BOLIVIA

A giant prehistoric saltwater lake, Lago Minchin, once covered most of south-western Bolivia before it dried up more than 10,000 years ago. What it left behind was one of the world's most unusual panoramic views in the form of a gigantic salt flat, Earth's largest, which at 4,086 square miles in area, is bigger than the nations of Cyprus and Lebanon and almost three times the size of Guam.

Found high in the Altiplano of Bolivia, 12,000 feet above sea level, Salar de Uyuni is almost perfectly flat, with a maximum deviation across its entire extent of just three feet. Coupled with the strikingly clear skies that exist most of the year, it is no surprise that the flats are exploited by space satellites, bouncing signals off its surface, to calibrate their altitude in space down to inches of accuracy. At certain times of the year, nearby lakes overflow and a thin layer of water transforms the flats into a striking 80 mile-wide mirror – a perfect, shimmering canvas for trick photography and mirror images of the flats and sky.

Salar de Uyuni's chief industry besides tourism is salt mining. Salt deposits extend more than 30 feet deep in places and are mined locally by a workers' cooperative who form heaped cones of salt scraped out of the flats' surface to dry out in the sun. More than 10 billion tons of salt are contained in the flats along with as much as half the world's reserves of lithium. Little plant life exists in this barren region, but every November, the flats are transformed into a riot of color as three species of flamingo arrive to breed.

Salar De Uyuni, Bolivia.

Salt piles on Salar De Uyuni's salt flats.

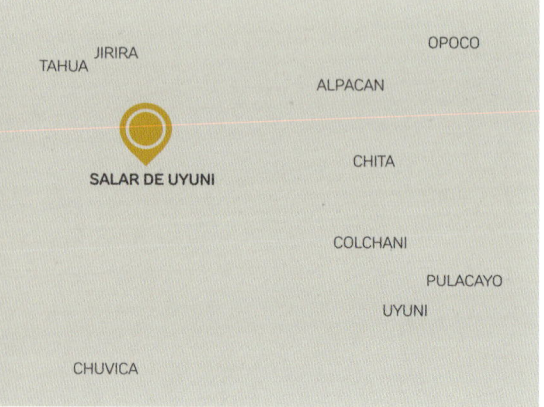

TAHUA
JIRIRA
OPOCO
ALPACAN
SALAR DE UYUNI
CHITA
COLCHANI
PULACAYO
UYUNI
CHUVICA

Salar de Uyuni is the world's largest salt flat

Torres Del Paine National Park, Patagonia, Chile

Guanaco in Torres del Paine National Park

TORRES DEL PAINE NATIONAL PARK

PATAGONIA, CHILE

Despite its relative isolation at the southern tip of South America, more than a quarter of a million people trek to this end of the Andes annually. There, they experience the Patagonian region of Chile's incredibly rugged beauty only equalled by its diversity. Landscapes vary from arid, cold desert to fast-flowing whitewater rivers, open steppe grassland and wooded glades and valleys, above which regal Andean condors with their 10–11 feet wingspans often soar. Amongst the park's 448,280 acres lie four different vegetation zones – including Andean Desert scrub grasses and shrubs, and subpolar forest with deciduous Antarctic beech trees, which line many of the park's most prominent gorges.

At the height of the southern hemisphere summer, visitors are treated to more than 17 hours of sunlight, beginning early in the morning with the sun alighting on the granite horns of the Torres massif, coloring them in impressive shades of red and purple. The sun sweeps over the park's many scenic lakes including Lake Pehoé and the 12.6 square miles of Grey Lake, which is fed by a glacier of the same name and often contains stunning giant icebergs.

The grey glacier at Torres Del Paine National Park, Patagonia, Chile

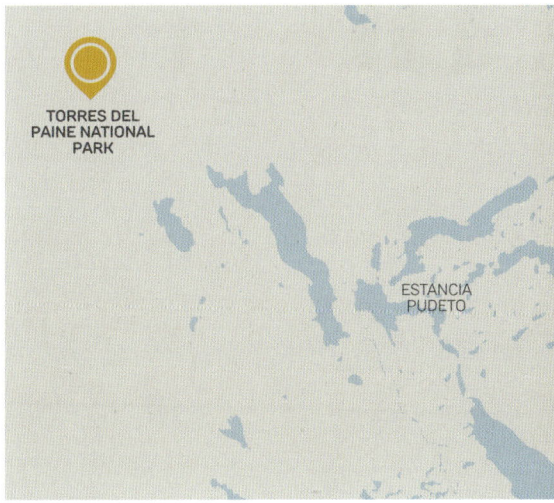
TORRES DEL PAINE NATIONAL PARK

ESTÁNCIA PUDETO

MONTEVERDE CLOUD FOREST

COSTA RICA

This Central American paradise is a wild world of dense vegetation shrouded in perpetual rain and mist. Cloud forests are rare and precious. They occur within tropical or subtropical mountainous environments where almost constant cloud cover reduces the rate of evaporation, keeping moisture within the dense forest and stimulating vibrant plant growth including more species of orchid than anywhere on Earth.

A reserve of just 810 acres was established in this part of the Cordillera de Tilarán mountain range in northern Costa Rica in 1972. It has since expanded to over 35,000 acres with elevations ranging from 2,000 to over 6,000 feet. Visitors have more than eight miles of trails they can hike through as well as a network of eight hanging bridges suspended high above the forest floor in the Selvatura Park region.

Monteverde is one of the planet's greatest biodiversity hotspots containing over 120 species of amphibians and reptiles and 58 different types of bats as well as margays, howler monkeys, pumas, and jaguars, the latter often spotted resting in lower tree branches or prowling the forest floor. In addition, there are 400 species of bird including the magnificent resplendent quetzal and the rare and endangered three-wattled bellbird. According to the Cloud Forest Reserve that oversees this wild wonderland, Monteverde makes up just one fifth of one percent of Costa Rica's total land area, yet it holds a staggering 50 percent of all its different flora and fauna.

SANTE ELENA

MONTE VERDE

MONTEVERDE
CLOUD FOREST

Monteverde cloud forest, Costa Rica.

Sunset on Ipanema beach, Rio De Janeiro.

Ipanema beach, Rio De Janeiro.

IPANEMA BEACH

RIO DE JANEIRO, BRAZIL

Stretching between Arpoador and Leblon beaches, this is where many of Rio de Janeiro's inhabitants come out to pose and play, basking on the sun-drenched white sands or frolicking in its warm sea whose swell, strong undertow, and, at times, waves reaching nine feet in height, help give it its indigenous name from the Tupi language, meaning, "bad, dangerous waters".

Tourists flock to chill out or gawp at the parade of bronzed bodies strutting, preening, playing, watching, and relaxing. Beach lifeguard stations known as *postos* (posts) informally divide Rio's beaches into distinct parts. Post 10, for example, is a magnet for sporty Brazilians with many games of beach volleyball, soccer on the sand, or *frescobol* (beach tennis using a rubber ball and wooden bats) are played.

Synonymous with the Brazilian beach scene, Ipanema was made world-famous when it spawned the lilting bossa nova hit, 'Girl From Ipanema', written by two local musicians in 1962. Traces of the beach's past as a hangout for hippies remain with counter-culturalists tending to group round Post 9 and a flea market first held in 1968, Feira Hippie de Ipanema, still held today and containing as many as 700 stalls.

BOTAFOGO

HUMAITÁ

LAGOA

COPACABANA

IPANEMA

Ipanema beach, Rio De Janeiro.

GREAT BLUE HOLE
BELIZE

This collapsed cave system prompts pilgrimages of around 200,000 sightseers a year, despite being a two-hour boat ride away from the coast of the Central American nation of Belize. It is located in Lighthouse Reef some 62 miles from Belize City and started out around 153,000 years ago as a limestone cave system which was flooded by rising water levels. This caused the cave roof to collapse and a giant sinkhole to form, far deeper than the surrounding waters, which is what gives the hole its distinctive and mysterious dark blue color.

The hole spans a width of 984 feet and measures around 407–410 feet deep. Caves line some parts of its walls, some of which contain giant stalactites reaching more than 25 feet in length.
The first scientific investigation of the Great Blue Hole was performed by French underwater exploration icon, Jacques Cousteau, and his team, in 1971. Cousteau's film of the team's dives, part of *The Underwater World of Jacques Cousteau* TV series, popularised the Great Blue Hole, which became a popular dive site as a result. Whilst midnight parrotfish, anemones, and other marine life can be found inside the hole, more species, including giant groupers and nurse and hammerhead sharks, are found around its edges which are now fringed by coral reefs.

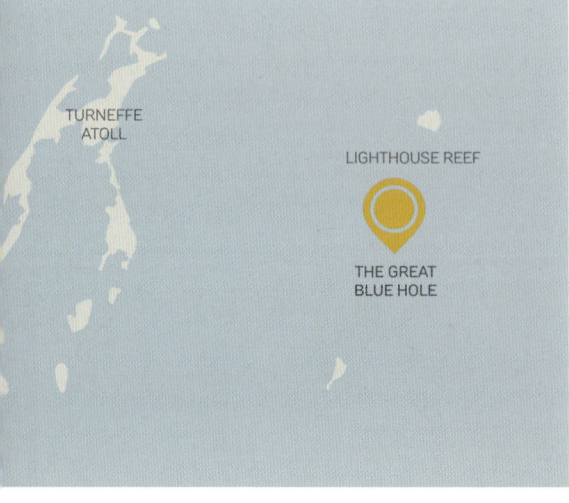

TURNEFFE ATOLL

LIGHTHOUSE REEF

THE GREAT BLUE HOLE

Great Blue Hole, Belize.

TIKAL

GUATEMALA

Some 190 miles north of the country's capital city lies a powerful symbol of the pre-Columbian Maya civilization's skill, aesthetic prowess and organization. Lying inside a national park whose 220 square miles are mostly deep, dense jungle, is this ancient city hewn out of limestone blocks and comprising more than 3,000 buildings and structures.

Inhabited in some form or other for a span of 1,500 years, Tikal is thought to have reached its peak between 200 CE and 800 CE during which time its stunning steep-sided temples were constructed. The Temple of the Great Jaguar, for example, reaches a height of 154 feet yet is towered over by the 230-foot-high Temple of the Double-Headed Serpent, one of the tallest ancient buildings in the Americas. Many of the city's structures, including dozens of stelae columns, are beautifully carved with hieroglyphic symbols and representations of people or gods, a captivating sight for lovers of history.

The lush rainforest has been cleared from the core of the city revealing a high degree of planning and foresight involved in laying out the city's attractive broad causeways and plazas, its palace complexes and other structures. Yet, the jungle never remains far from view and with it the piercing cries of the abundant birdlife and monkeys beneath the rainforest canopy.

TIKAL

CRUCE DOS AGUADAS

EL CAOBA
SAN ROMAN
SAN JOSE   LAKE   EL REMATE
SAN ANDRÉS   PETÉN ITZÁ   EL CRUCE
       MACANCHE

FLORES
SAN BENITO
LA PONDEROSA

Tikal, Guatemala.

TEOTIHUACAN

MEXICO

Just 30 miles northeast of Mexico City lies a stunning former imperial capital which reached its peak around 1,550 years ago as the greatest city in the Americas. Whilst little is known about the Mesoamerican culture who constructed this ancient wonder, its grandeur and monumental beauty can still be appreciated up close.

The name given to this city, meaning, "the city where Gods were made," actually comes from a far later civilization, the Aztecs, who were awestruck by its scale. With an area of some 8–9 square miles, the city was bigger than ancient Rome or Athens. Sophisticated city planning was at work throughout with broad avenues, monumental religious buildings, large numbers of artisanal workshops and quarters, and two enormous public spaces, named by archaeologists as the Great Compound and the Citadel, the latter a sunken square around the size of 18 full-sized soccer pitches.

The city's alignment demonstrates the culture's astronomical prowess. Its biggest building, the 733 foot long and wide Temple of the Sun, for example, is aligned to the locations of various sunrises and sunsets on specific dates of the year. Looting and other ravages of time have stripped the city of the bright murals believed to have adorned many building walls, but artefacts that remain prove that this ancient settlement was peopled by great artists and craftworkers, proficient in jade, stone sculpting and painted art.

SAN AGUSTÍN ACTIPAC   SANTA MARÍA PALAPA

SAN ANTONIO DE LAS PALMAS

SAN MARTÍN DE LAS PIRÁMIDES

SAN JUAN TEOTIHUACÁN

SAN SEBASTIÁN XOLALPA

SAN LORENZO TLALMIMILOLPAN

SANTIAGO ATLATONGO

SAN BARTOLO

ACOLMAN   XOMETLA

Teotihuacan, Mexico.

View of seven Ahu Akivi Moai, which are the only Moai to face the sea. Rapa Nui, Easter Island.

Aerial view of Rano Kau volcano on Rapa Nui, Easter Island.

EASTER ISLAND
PACIFIC OCEAN

Beauty comes in many forms and to many, the bleak but powerful vistas of this largely treeless island all on its own in the South Pacific can compete with the riches found elsewhere. One key reason is found dotted all over the island in the form of more than 880 monumental *moai* statues, their brooding faces with high foreheads and long noses, just like the island itself, shrouded in mystery.

A single volcanic crater, Rano Raraku, was quarried to produce the 500–900 year old statues, cut as one piece directly out of the interior crater face, and all without metal tools. The largest part-finished statue, El Gigante, would have stood 69 feet tall and weighed over 150 tons – the weight of three fully-loaded Boeing 737-100 airliners. These were then transported all over the island, mostly to coastal locations where they were mounted on ceremonial platforms called *ahu* and topped with a *pukao* hair knot carved out of red scoria stone.

Many questions abound, from why the statues were constructed and later toppled to how Polynesians settled one of the world's most isolated isles, more than 2,000 miles away from significant landmasses in any direction, and what their writings, in a unique and, so far, indecipherable script known as *rongorongo*, state. It is these mysteries and the haunting beauty of the statues' inscrutable faces that make Easter Island a place like no other.

EASTER ISLAND

HANGA ROA

Moais on the slope of Rano Raraku volcano, Rapa Nui Easter Island.

Smoky Mountains, Appalachian range, USA.

NORTH AMERICA

HAWAII / WYOMING / ARIZONA / CANADA / NEW MEXICO / ALASKA
/ SAN FRANCISCO /UTAH / COLORADO / CALIFORNIA

GRAND CANYON
ARIZONA, USA

Millions of Americans and foreign visitors flock to Arizona each year to visit this majestic canyon gouged deep into the Earth's surface. Few are disappointed. The mighty, fast-flowing Colorado River transported vast quantities of stones, gravel, and sediment in its waters which acted as a powerful abrasive, scouring and cutting the surrounding rocks. Over millions of years, a giant winding canyon was formed measuring 277 miles long and between 500 feet to 18 miles wide along its great length. In places, it reaches a depth of more than 1.1 miles. Overall, it spans an area bigger than Rhode Island.

The erosive power of the Colorado River's waters has not only sculpted rock stacks; over 330 identified caves (and possibly many more) and other rock formations can also be found in the canyon. Only one cave is open and accessible – the Cave of the Domes on Horseshoe Mesa. The river also cut deep into the Earth's crust, revealing a striking cross section of differing rock strata, from three of the four geological eras of Earth's existence. The oldest date back more than 1.5 billion years giving geologists unprecedented looks back in time at how the landscape formed.

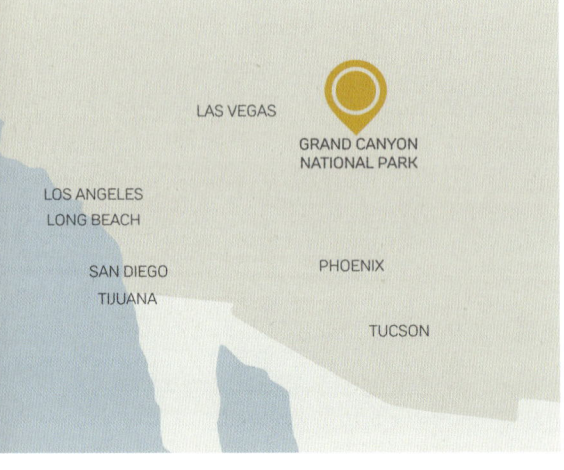

LAS VEGAS

GRAND CANYON
NATIONAL PARK

LOS ANGELES
LONG BEACH

SAN DIEGO
TIJUANA

PHOENIX

TUCSON

Grand Canyon, Arizona.

In **1869, the first successful trip through the entire Grand Canyon was taken in rowing boats** commanded by John Wesley Powell, a one-armed US Civil War veteran. Visitor interest in the canyon increased during the late 19th century with US President Theodore Roosevelt declaring in 1903 that it was "one of the great sights every American should see." He established the Grand Canyon Game Preserve three years later, urging people to "Leave it as it is. You cannot improve on it. The ages have been at work on it, and man can only mar it." In 1919, the canyon, and the area surrounding it, was made a national park. Just 44,173 people visited it in the park's first year. Today, that figure is closer to 5.9 million.

More than 200 species of bird and over 50 different mammals including skunks, raccoons, coyotes, and bats are found in the park whilst discovered artefacts proved how ancient peoples lived in the canyon as far back as 12,000 years ago. Around 1,000 years ago, the Hisatsinom or Anasazi native Americans lived and farmed the canyon floor, growing corn, beans and squash along the banks of the river. One of the greatest viewpoints over the canyon is the aptly-dubbed The Skywalk, managed by the Hualapai Native American people. It consists of a horseshoe shaped steel frame with glass floor and sides that projects about 70 feet over the rim of the canyon.

A calm stretch on the Colorado River in the Grand Canyon, Arizona.

Toroweap Overlook on the north rim of the Grand Canyon National Park, Arizona.

" You cannot see the Grand Canyon in one view, as if it were a changeless spectacle from which a curtain might be lifted, but to see it, you have to toil from month to month through its labyrinths. "

John Wesley Powell, American explorer and geologist.

unset over the Grand Canyon National Park, Arizona.

HORSESHOE BEND

ARIZONA, USA

Around four miles southwest of the Arizona town of Page, lies a stretch of the Colorado River which is a prime example of the power of water to follow the line of least resistance yet with the capability to sculpt hard, unyielding rock to its will. This 270-degree U-bend in the river's route, known as an incised or entrenched meander, is the eventual result of tectonic plate movement uplifting the Colorado Plateau around 20 million years ago, according to the US Geological Service. As the land rose, waters responded by cutting ever deeper and wider stream and river channels into the surrounding rock.

Horseshoe Bend has become a magnet for social media posts, resulting in a great increase in visitors clambering up the sandy path to experience its magnificence from the bend's rim and to peer down the steep walls in wonder at the 1,000-foot drop to the river below. It's a stirring site for, as photographer Ryan Houston states, "At this viewpoint, you can see the waters of the Colorado River in all their sparkling, blue-green glory as they drift along toward the Grand Canyon."

HORSESHOE BEND

LAS VEGAS

GRAND CANYON NATIONAL PARK

LOS ANGELES
LONG BEACH

SAN DIEGO

PHOENIX

TIJUANA

TUCSON

Horseshoe Bend, Arizona

NIAGARA FALLS

CANADA / USA

Geologically young at 12,000 years old, these falls thunder with undreamt of force as the river's waters make their way between two of the Great Lakes (Erie and Ontario). A deep gorge scoured through the landscape has resulted in three sets of falls: The 2,200-foot-wide Horseshoe Falls lie mostly within Canadian territory whilst both American Falls and Bridal Falls are within New York state.

When the river flows fullest and fiercest, as much as 100,000 cubic feet of water plummets over the falls every second. The water drops more than 150 feet, making a thunderous noise and generating thick mist and frequent rainbows. The constantly cascading water erodes the underlying dolomite and shale rock bed and as a result, the falls are receding back up the river at a current rate of around one foot a year, just a third of the historical average.

Members of Samuel De Champlain's expedition to Canada became the first Europeans to encounter the falls as early as 1604. Niagara became a magnet for early explorers and travellers including John Franklin who, on his second Arctic expedition in 1825, praised the falls as, "so justly

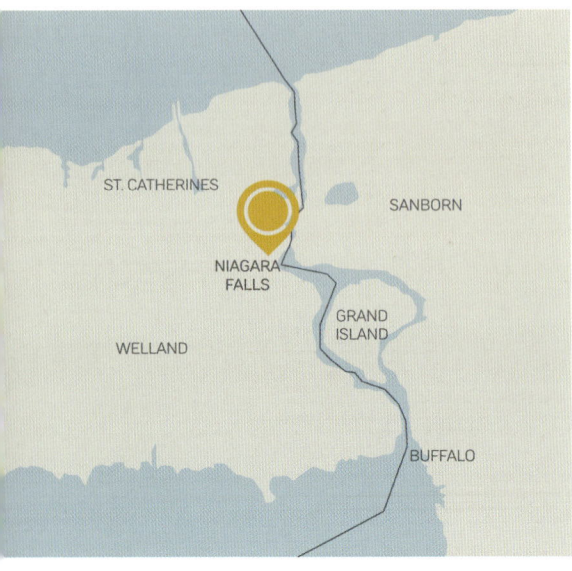

Niagara Falls, Canada.

celebrated as the first in the world for grandeur." Sixty years later, the Niagara Falls State Park – America's oldest state park – was established to protect some 400 acres of land surrounding the river and falls.

The crashing water attracts in excess of eight million visitors each year, prompting the development of sizeable communities on both sides of the border. Numerous vantage points exist to cope with the demand including Goat Island in the middle of the river, and Rainbow Bridge, which connects the two nations by road. Hydroelectric power plants on both sides of the river exploit the falls to generate vast amounts of electricity – around 4.4 gigawatts or enough to provide energy to more than 2 million homes. Niagara has also proven a magnet for daredevils from high-wire stuntman Nik Wallenda, who made a 1,800 foot tightrope walk across the falls in 2012, to Annie Edson Taylor, a 63 year old ex-schoolteacher who became the first to survive a trip over the falls in a wooden barrel, 111 years earlier.

Aerial view of Niagara Falls, Canada.

Niagara Falls, Canada.

66 Their roar is around me. I am on the brink
Of the great waters - and their anthem voice
Goes up amid the rainbow and the mist. 99

– extract from 'Niagara', an 1839 poem by Grenville Mellen.

Niagara Falls frozen in the winter.

The Dolls Theater, Carlsbad Cavern, New Mexico.

Stalactites hang from the cave roof inside Carlsbad Cavern.

CARLSBAD CAVERN

CHIHUAHUA DESERT, NEW MEXICO

"I found myself gazing into the biggest and blackest hole I had ever seen, out of which the bats seemed literally to boil," – the words of Texan-born teenager James Larkin White who around 1898 discovered an enormous network of caves, caverns and passageways under the Chihuahua Desert in New Mexico. Its deepest accessible cave floors are at a depth equivalent to an 80 story building underground.

The limestone reef from which the caverns were carved was laid down by a prehistoric inland sea around 255 million years ago. Water carrying sediment has built up extraordinary cave features including giant hanging stalactites, folded curtains, knobbly popcorn formations and the Giant Dome, a 16-foot diameter stalagmite that towers the height of ten men up from the cavern floor. The Big Room is Carlsbad's largest chamber. Its 357,469 square feet could comfortably accommodate six gridiron fields with ease.

Damage at the hands of miners of mineral-rich bat guano and treasure speculators sparked conservation campaigns that led to the cave system becoming a national monument in 1923 and a national park seven years later. Public access is limited to many of the caves as a result. The bats that James White referred to roost in the caverns during the warmer late spring and winter months. According to the National Parks Conservancy Association, 400,000 Brazilian free-tailed bats make their home there and all exit at sunset, creating yet another extraordinary sight at the caverns.

Carlsbad Cavern, New Mexico.

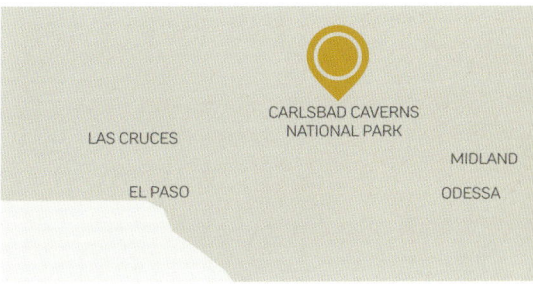

LAS CRUCES

CARLSBAD CAVERNS NATIONAL PARK

MIDLAND

EL PASO

ODESSA

DENALI

ALASKA, USA

In 1794, a report from British sailor George Vancouver talked of "stupendous snow mountains" spotted during his expedition. One of these proved to be Denali – the North American continent's highest peak with an elevation of 20,310 feet. The mountain is located approximately 170 miles southwest of Fairbanks and 130 miles north-northwest of Anchorage. It is situated in 4.7 million acres of national park alongside 1.3 million acres of national preserve – together about the same size as Vermont. One sixth of this landscape is covered in glaciers whilst the remainder contains almost 12,000 lakes, one of which, Wonder Lake, provides mirror-like reflections of the mountain and its imposing faces and jagged ridges.

Denali is an example of nature at its finest but also its harshest. Temperatures can drop below minus 70 °F which with wind chill can take it down as low as minus 118 °F enough to freeze unprotected body parts in mere seconds. Numerous attempts to scale the summit have ended in failure or disaster and only around half of those who attempt to bag this peak succeed. Thirty years after the United States purchased Alaska from Russia, a Princeton graduate turned gold prospector, William Dickey, named the mountain after the newly elected president, William McKinley, in a *New York Sun* article. The name was popularized after McKinley's assassination in 1901 and stuck until 2015 when the mountain returned to its former indigenous name meaning, "the Great One".

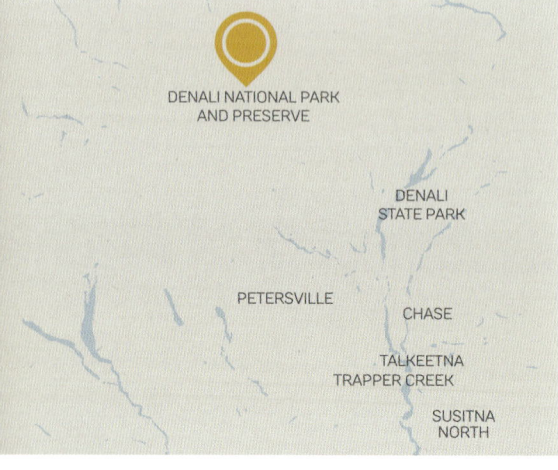

DENALI NATIONAL PARK AND PRESERVE

DENALI STATE PARK

PETERSVILLE

CHASE

TALKEETNA
TRAPPER CREEK

SUSITNA NORTH

Denali, Alaska.

Sunlight streams in only for a short period either side of midday, illuminating the canyon.

Colorful swirls of sedimentary sandstone form the curved walls within the canyon.

ANTELOPE CANYON

ARIZONA, USA

Small in scale but large in impact, Antelope Canyon is a peculiar pair of thin, twisting passages through rock. This pair of slot canyons are officially dubbed Upper and Lower Canyon but are just as well known by their nicknames of the Crack and the Corkscrew. A ten minute drive out of Page, Arizona, these twin canyons are dwarfed by their far bigger brother, the Grand Canyon, two hours away, but exhibit the same fascination for how erosion over time can produce extraordinary formations. Both are the results of the action of water on rock but flash floods here and the peculiar arrangement of the sedimentary sandstone have yielded a landscape of rock more out of a dream than reality.

Upper Canyon measures 660 feet in length and is shaped like an inverted V. There's plenty of room to clamber around but little light as sunlight streams in only for a short period either side of midday, illuminating the heady swirls of red, pink and orange colors found in the layers of rock. Lower Canyon is more than double the length of its cousin and more claustrophobic with the rock closing in at its base. Its floor is reached by a series of ladders some 120 feet down, from where its rippling waves of sculpted rock can be most impressively experienced.

The winding passages within the Antelope Canyon, Arizona.

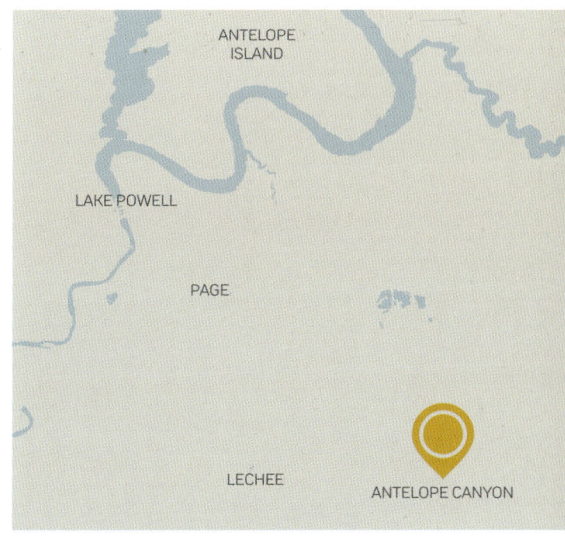

ANTELOPE ISLAND

LAKE POWELL

PAGE

LECHEE

ANTELOPE CANYON

MORAINE LAKE
ALBERTA, CANADA

Canada is home to more lakes than any other nation – two million in total, according to Natural Resources Canada. These cover almost nine percent of the country and many, including Lake Louise and Emerald, Peyto and Maligne lakes are world renowned. So, it takes a very special place to finish above these and others at the top of many travellers' surveys of the most beautiful water courses in Canada.

Located in Banff, Canada's oldest national park, Moraine Lake covers just 0.39 square miles in area but almost looks too perfect to be real. It lies at an elevation of 6,183 feet in the Valley of the Ten Peaks with the pinnacles of those ten mountains, all between 10,000 and 11,236 feet in height, framing the waters below and reflected in its surface. Fed by surrounding glaciers, the lake's water is both icy cold and appears a glittering turquoise color, in part caused by the high levels of fine glacial silt, known as rock flour washed into the lake. Hiking trails around its shoreline offer a variety of viewpoints to savor as well as opportunities to spot abundant wildlife including elk, moose, bighorn sheep, and, in the summer months, black and grizzly bears.

OLDS

BANFF NATIONAL
PARK OF CANADA

GOLDEN

MORAINE LAKE BANFF

AIRDRIE

CALGARY

CANMORE

OKOTOKS

RADIUM
HOT SPRINGS

HIGH RIVER

INVERMERE

Moraine Lake, Canada.

GOLDEN GATE BRIDGE

SAN FRANCISCO, USA

For more than two centuries, passing Spanish ships failed to spot San Francisco Bay, which was finally discovered by overland hunters in 1769. The Golden Gate Strait which links the bay to the Pacific was spanned by this, the world's longest suspension bridge, when it opened in 1937. Standing 746 feet tall and with its main span stretching 4,200 feet, the bridge was a triumph of American engineering, with approximately 600,000 rivets in each of its main towers and 80,000 miles of galvanised steel wire making up 27,572 strands in each of its main cables. These travel over the towers and are embedded in concrete at either end of the bridge.

More than just an engineering national icon, this majestic suspension bridge captivates those who cross it or view it from the banks, aided by consulting architect, Irving Morrow's decision to reject grey or black as its paint color, favoring "international orange" instead. As San Francisco newspaper columnist Herb Caen wrote so poignantly in 1987, "The mystical structure, with its perfect amalgam of delicacy and power, exerts an uncanny effect. Its efficiency cannot conceal the artistry. There is heart there, and soul. It is an object to be contemplated for hours."

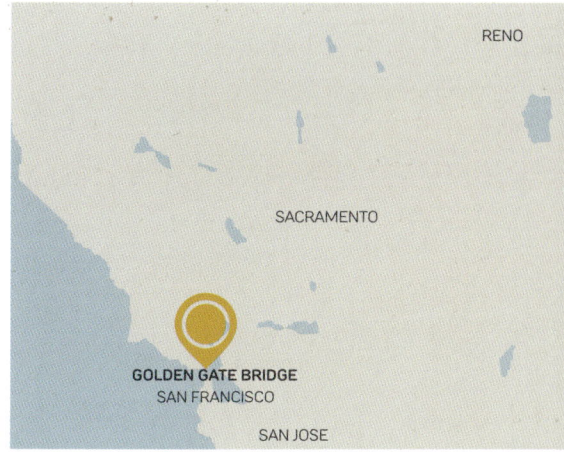

RENO

SACRAMENTO

GOLDEN GATE BRIDGE
SAN FRANCISCO

SAN JOSE

Sunrise over the Golden Gate Bridge, San Francisco.

BRYCE CANYON

UTAH, USA

Named after one of the early Mormon pioneers who settled this region of southwestern Utah, this series of bowls or amphitheatres carved out of the rock of a high elevation plateau form a geological wonderland. Slot canyons, precipitous cliffs, rocky fins and windows mix with the park's most famous feature, its vast collection of hoodoos – irregular and twisted rock columns and spires. Shaped over long periods of time through frost weathering, the hoodoos form one of the most surreal scenes found anywhere in the United States.

Numerous viewpoints along the 50 miles of trails within the park offer striking outlooks, especially just after dawn and before dusk. The word hoodoo means "to bewitch" and, when crested with snow in winter or viewed under the softer light of the rising or setting sun, the differing shapes and colors of the hoodoos, some standing ten stories tall, really do bewitch and entrance. A wide range of wildlife can also be found within the park's boundaries, from mule deer to mountain lions and marmots, whilst a look upwards may spot some of the 160 different bird species sometimes found within the park's boundaries including yellow rumped warblers, Steller's jay, and graceful peregrine falcons.

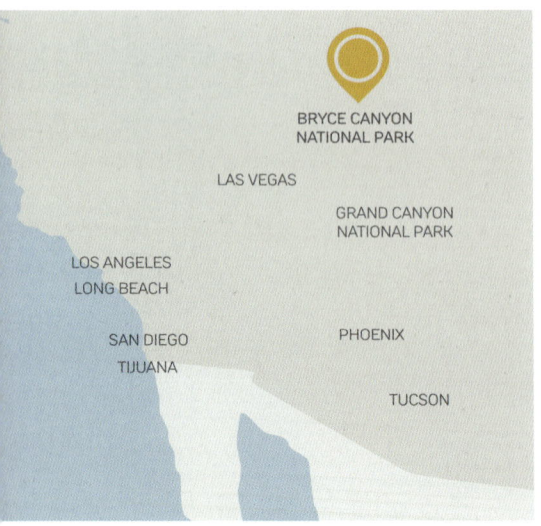

BRYCE CANYON
NATIONAL PARK

LAS VEGAS

GRAND CANYON
NATIONAL PARK

LOS ANGELES
LONG BEACH

SAN DIEGO
TIJUANA

PHOENIX

TUCSON

Colours and formations of the Bryce Canyon National Park

THE MAROON BELLS

COLORADO, USA

Colorado's Elk Mountains contain six 'fourteeners' — peaks over 14,000 feet in elevation. Amongst them stand these super scenic twin mountains, one of the state's and, indeed, nation's most photographed sites. Located just ten miles west of the resort of Aspen, the rocky peaks are contrasted by the forested valleys and lower slopes below, home to mule deer and marmots amongst other creatures. Many visitors time their arrival in September to coincide with the leaves on the large swathes of aspen forest below the peak turning from green to a rich autumnal gold.

At 14,163 feet, Maroon Peak is just 144 feet taller than its sister, North Maroon Peak and separated from it at its summit by just a short distance. Unusually in the Rockies, whose pinnacles are usually constructed of limestone or robust granite, the Maroon peaks are made of mudstone which flakes and is prone to landslides. These peaks began their formation some 300 million years ago from the accretion of sediment caused by the erosion of former granite based mountain ranges — the Uncompahgre Mountains and the Ancestral Front Range. Oxidation of minerals within the sediment gives the mountains their reddish hues from which their name is derived.

Sunrise at The Maroon Bells.

FORT COLLINS

DENVER

GRAND JUNCTION

THE MAROON BELLS

COLORADO SPRINGS

PUEBLO

THE WAVE
ARIZONA / UTAH, USA

Rock formations rarely get more unusual or other-worldly than the extraordinarily twisted and flowing layers of sedimentary rocks found on the border of Arizona and Utah. The twisting ravine is made up of two troughs, the largest measuring 62 feet wide and over 118 feet long, formed from 180 million year old Jurassic sand dunes compacted into rock. Successive spells of erosion, water, then wind have helped create the formation's sweeping, swirling curves whilst varying levels of iron oxide in the layers of sand resulted in a rainbow of yellow, pink and red layers that give the Wave its striking, striped colors

Standing in the midst of the Wave as light streams down at midday makes many visitors feel like lottery winners, which in essence they are. Because of the fragility of the rock formations, as well as their scientific and cultural value, the Bureau of Land Management heavily restricts access to the area, issuing only twenty permits for entry per day, via online and write-in lotteries.

The Wave is located inside Vermilion Cliffs National Monument, which hosts sideshows of further strange sandstone formations including steep-sided buttes and stone hoodoo columns as well as trails of 190 million year old dinosaur footprints, numbering in excess of 1,000 tracks.

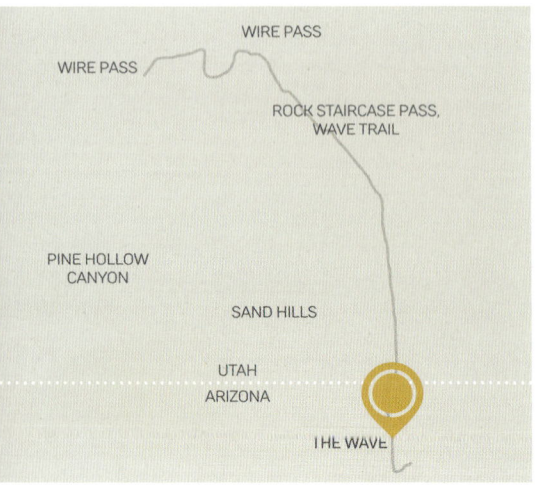

Coyote Buttes in the Paria Canyon..

The Wave at Paria Canyon, Vermilion Cliffs National Monument.

The twisting and flowing layers of Coyote Buttes, Paria Canyon.

EMERALD LAKE

YOHO NATIONAL PARK, CANADA

The name Yoho comes from the Cree native American word for awe and wonder and the largest of this national park's 61 lakes certainly inspires those emotions. It was first called Emerald Lake on account of the striking color of its waters by a Canadian guide, Tom Wilson - the first non-native to encounter the lake in 1882. It wasn't the first lake Wilson had named thus. Earlier that year he had discovered a lake 25 miles away to the east, which has since been renamed Lake Louise and is located within neighboring Banff National Park.

Emerald Lake freezes over for half of the year, usually beginning in November. As the ice recedes the lake's waters retain glacier silt in suspension which scatters light and helps give the waters their remarkable jade-to-turquoise coloration. This jewel in the Canadian Rockies stands at an elevation of 4,265 feet - lower in comparison to many other lakes in the region. As a result, it thaws a little earlier, typically from the middle of May onwards, allowing visitors to hike round its trails and enjoy the abundance of western hemlock, red cedar and pine that fringe the lake.

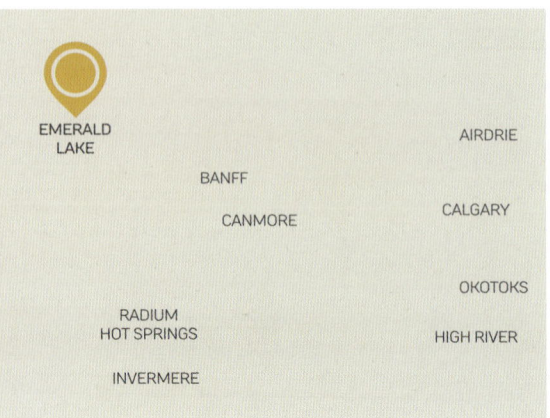

EMERALD LAKE

AIRDRIE

BANFF

CANMORE

CALGARY

OKOTOKS

RADIUM HOT SPRINGS

HIGH RIVER

INVERMERE

The reflective waters of the Emerald Lake, Yoho National Park.

YOSEMITE NATIONAL PARK
CALIFORNIA, USA

America's third national park, Yosemite, is found in the heart of the Sierra Nevada mountain range. With its forested slopes and valleys, gushing creeks and imposing granite rock formations, it is a wilderness paradise. Although the Yosemite Valley makes up only one hundredth of the park's 1,189 square miles, it is where most of the 4–5 million annual visitors head. There they will find noteworthy features such as Sentinel Peak, the Bridalveil Falls and the giant, domed slab of granite named El Capitan after an Ahwahnechee chief. Its 3,000-foot-high vertical walls throw down a challenge that many experienced rock climbers cannot resist taking on.

With much of its area rarely troubled by human activity, the park is a haven for wildlife including mountain lions, 300–500 black bears and 17 species of bats. In the southern part of the park lies Mariposa Grove, where visitors can get up close and personal with a full square mile of towering giant sequoia trees. Amongst them stands the Grizzly Giant, which stands 209 feet tall and is estimated by the National Parks Service at 1,800 years of age. The grove was first discovered and conserved by Galen Clark who in 1866 was made the first park guardian to protect its natural treasures for future generations.

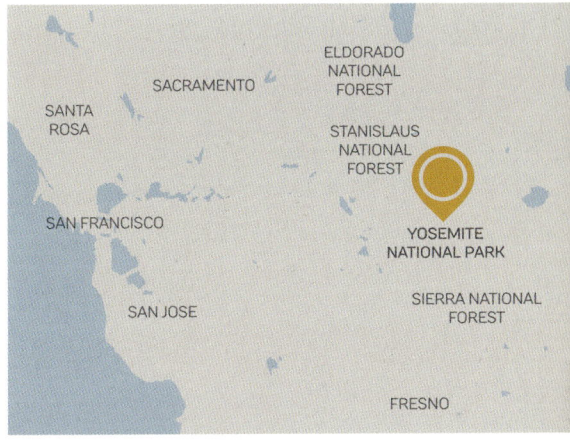

Breathtaking sunrise over Yosemite National Park.

GRAND PRISMATIC SPRING

YELLOWSTONE NATIONAL PARK, USA

Wyoming's Yellowstone Park became America's first National Park back in 1872. This mountain wilderness region is a treasure trove of natural wonders and provides homes for more than 150 species of bird as well as elk, bison, mountain lions and black and grizzly bears amongst its more than 60 species of mammals.

Yellowstone is located over a hot spot — a part of the Earth's crust where incredibly hot molten rock, called magma, is close to the surface. As a result, the park contains many steam vents where hot steam rises from below the Earth's surface as well as bubbling pools of hot mud, hot springs, and geysers. The most famous geyser is Old Faithful, which erupts some 20 times a day. Each eruption sends a spray of heated water and vapor between 100 and 180 feet into the air and typically lasts between one and a half to five minutes.

CANYON VILLAGE

WEST YELLOWSTONE

GRAND PRISMATIC SPRING

YELLOWSTONE LAKE

BIG SPRINGS

CARIBOU-TARGHEE NATIONAL FOREST

Access along a boardwalk gives visitors a close-up view of the Grand Prismatic Spring.

> **" The Grand Prismatic Hot Spring has been captivating visitors to the park since it was first viewed. "**

Douglas Scott, The Outdoor Society.

Whilst Old Faithful is the most famous, the Grand Prismatic Spring is Yellowstone's most photographed feature and with good reason. It is the largest hot spring in the United States and the third largest in the world behind New Zealand's Frying Pan Lake and Boiling Lake in Dominica. With a diameter of approximately 370 feet it is wider than a football field is long. A magnificent rainbow of colors surrounds the spring's center where water bubbles up 121 feet from underground chambers, heated by the hot rocks below to approximately 189 degrees Fahrenheit. At the center of the spring, little life can sustain itself in the fiercely hot waters, so the spring appears a deep blue. As the temperature drops on the outer rings of the spring, so more and varied bacteria live in its waters creating rings of light blues, greens, yellows, oranges and reds – a remarkable sight.

The spring was first examined scientifically in 1871 when the Hayden Expedition travelled to Wyoming. The expedition's leader, Ferdinand Hayden had nothing but praise for this extraordinary land feature, stating, "Nothing ever conceived by human art could equal the peculiar vividness and delicacy of color of these remarkable prismatic springs. Life becomes a privilege and a blessing after one has seen and thoroughly felt these incomparable types of nature's cunning skill."

This page, top: Mammoth Hot Springs, Yellowstone National Park.
This page, below: The colorful Grand Prismatic Spring (of Midway Geyser Basin), Yellowstone National Park.
Right page: An aerial shot of the colorful Grand Prismatic Spring.

The beautiful Nā Pali coastline

Hawaiian canoe on the beach at Hanalei pier at dawn.

NĀ PALI

HAWAII, USA

This seventeen-mile stretch of remote coast on Kaua'i, the Garden Isle, is named after its steep cliffs, some of which rise 4,000 feet above the churning ocean waters below. Originally formed through violent volcanic action, wind and water erosion has left its artistic mark on the landscape with jagged and fluted peaks sloping suddenly downwards towards the coast, which contains lava tubes, sea caves and deep, narrow valleys heavily forested in lush vegetation and often containing small waterfalls and streams.

The rugged terrain is little changed from the landscape that greeted the first arrivals to its shores at least 800 years ago. Historians believe that these voyagers were Polynesians whose ancestors braved more than 2,000 miles of Pacific Ocean in double-hulled outrigger sailing canoes to reach Hawaii. Ancient walled terraces can be found in some of Nā Pali's valleys where these early settlers grew taro, breadfruit and sweet potato. Nā Pali is now enclosed and protected in a 6,175 acre State Wilderness Park, and is home to the arduous but highly rewarding 11 mile Kalalau Trail from Haena to the Kalalau Valley and its small beach and waterfall - Ho'ole'a Falls.

Sun setting over Ke'e Beach, Kaua'i.

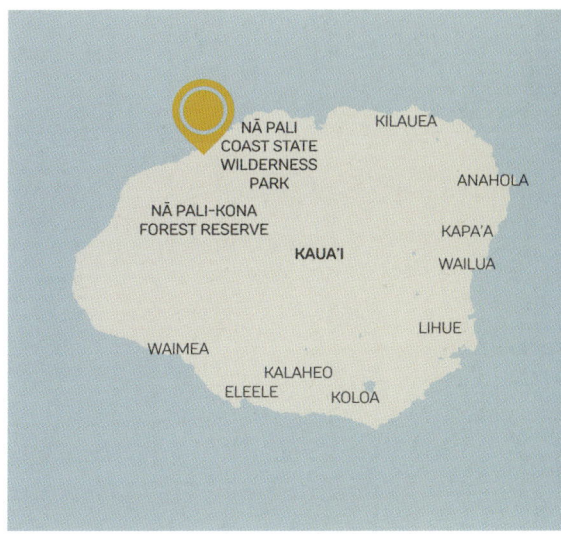

Flamingos in Lake Nakuru National Park Reserve, Kenya.

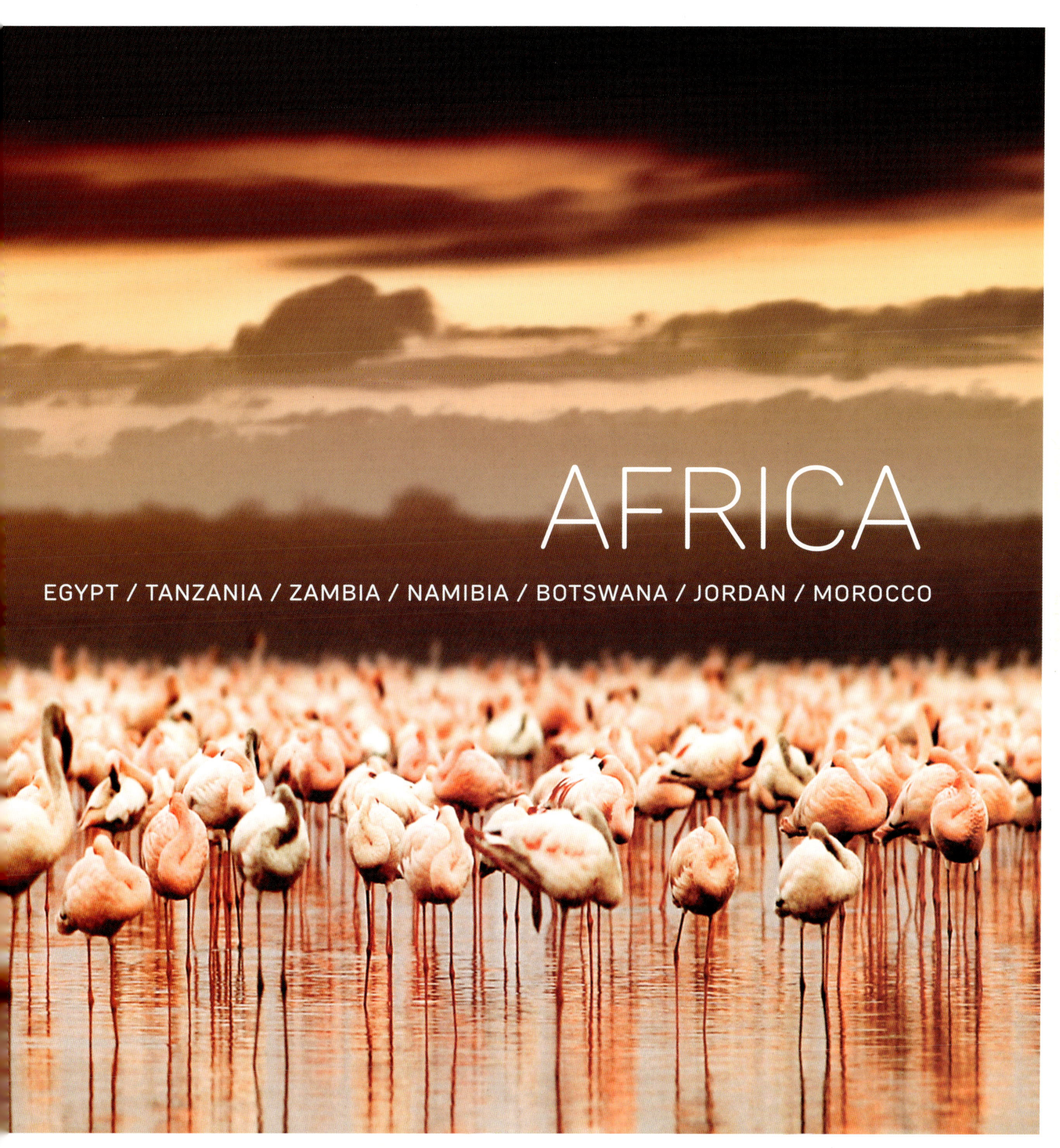

AFRICA

EGYPT / TANZANIA / ZAMBIA / NAMIBIA / BOTSWANA / JORDAN / MOROCCO

GREAT PYRAMID

GIZA, EGYPT

More than 110 stone pyramids, constructed in ancient Egypt, have been discovered, but only one comes with the epithet "Great". It is a matter of scale with the Great Pyramid dwarfing all others. When completed in around 2570 BCE and topped with a cap of glistening polished white limestone, it stood 481 feet high and remained the tallest building in the world for over 3,800 years until the completion of Lincoln Cathedral in 1311.

The Great Pyramid was built for fourth dynasty pharaoh Khufu and is a monument to the incredible heights reached by ancient Egyptian organization and endeavor. Each of its four faces measures 756 feet along their base, incline at an angle of 52 degrees and are aligned with the four cardinal compass points. An astonishing 2.3 million limestone blocks, with an average weight of 2.5 tons each, had to be quarried, cut, finished and hauled, all without the aid of the wheel, crane or other modern machinery we take for granted. Inside the monolith, a series of internal shafts and passageways led to chambers including a granite lined King's Chamber measuring 34.4 feet by 17.17 feet, deep inside the pyramid where the pharaoh's body once lay.

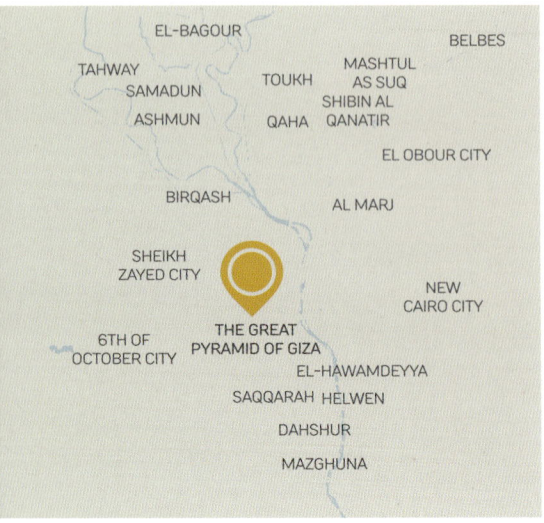

The Great Pyramid, Giza.

> *...the Great Pyramid, in all its unexpected bulk and majesty, towers close above one's head ... The effect is as sudden as it is overwhelming. It shuts out the sky and the horizon. It shuts out all the other Pyramids. It shuts out everything but the sense of awe and wonder.*

Amelia Blandford Edwards in her book,
A Thousand Miles Up the Nile, 1877

As many as 70,000 workers labored on the project for two decades. Historians once thought they were slaves but the discovery of a worker's village close by in the 1990s has revised our understanding and construction is now thought to have been largely by citizens of the kingdom performing their corvée – unpaid labor offered as tax payment. Although long since plundered of its shiny stone surface outside and its treasures inside, millions still flock to Giza for a chance to witness the last of the seven wonders of the ancient world still standing.

Khufu's pyramid is not alone. It is flanked by two large pyramids – the tombs of later fourth dynasty kings, Khafre and Menkaere, as well as three 20m high Queens' pyramids, believed to be for Khufu's wives and sisters. Close by is the enigmatic Great Sphinx – the 240 feet long recumbent lion with the head of an Egyptian king which has enraptured the world

A pit close to the pyramid was discovered in 1954 to contain 1,224 pieces of wood which turned out to be a 143-foot-long barge, made of cedar wood bound together by ropes. Reassembled painstakingly over many years, it is now on display in a facility next to the pyramid as a "masterpiece of woodcraft," and the world's oldest intact ship.

Close-up of the pyramids limestone bricks.

The Great Sphinx with the Pyramid of Menkaure in the background.

Many camels are used for transporting tourists to the pyramids.

VICTORIA FALLS
ZAMBIA, ZIMBABWE

Deep in the heart of Africa lies an enormous wall of water, spanning 1.25 miles, and forming the longest unbroken waterfall in the world. Locals called it *Mosi-oa-Tunya* (The Smoke that Thunders). British explorer David Livingstone, the first European to view the falls, named it after the British empire monarch of the time, Queen Victoria. He described the panoramic views as, "scenes so lovely must have been gazed upon by angels in their flight."

Created by the powerful Zambezi River as it flows from Zambia to Zimbabwe and empties into a series of narrow gorges, the falls plunge over the sharp lip of a plateau made of basalt and plummet up to 354 feet down into the waters below — more than twice the height of Niagara Falls. The bravest of visitors during the dry season (September to December) can obtain the most precipitous of views from the world's most extreme infinity pool, by bathing in the Devil's Pool right on the edge where a natural bowl-shaped depression of rock keeps them from being washed over.

During the wet season, in the early months of each year, so much water thunders over the edge (approximating to 20,000 bath tubs) that a mist of water vapor can rise over 1,300ft into the air and be viewed from up to two dozen miles away. At night, when there's a clear sky and a full moon, a 'moonbow' (lunar rainbow) can form through the mist.

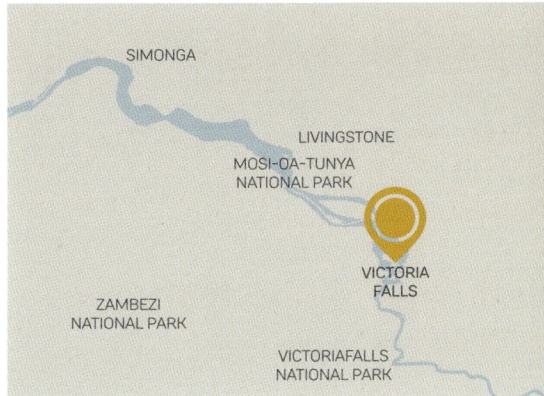

Sunset over Victoria Falls, on the Zambia / Zimbabwe border.

SERENGETI NATIONAL PARK

TANZANIA

This tract of classic African savannah, dotted with acacia trees, can seem wonderfully tranquil and serene on occasion, but it is also the location of the greatest mass migration on Earth. Close to two million mammals make an annual journey across the Serengeti's plains into the Masai Mara Game Reserve in Kenya in search of fresh grazing grounds. Precise timings are determined by rainfall, but the migration starts in the southwest Serengeti in late spring with the herds moving north and then east reaching the Masai Mara between August and October. The round trip is can be as much as 1,000 miles and witnessing any stage at close quarters is a remarkable sight.

Between 1.2 million and 1.7 million wildebeest make the journey, along with 12,000 eland, 350,000 gazelles and more than 200,000 zebra. These animals travel for protection in huge herds but are often shadowed by lions, leopards, cheetahs and hyenas awaiting their chance to strike whilst crocodiles lurk at river crossings for the unwary ungulates. Around a quarter of a million wildebeest perish along the way but offset by almost double that number of births enabling this endless cycle to continue.

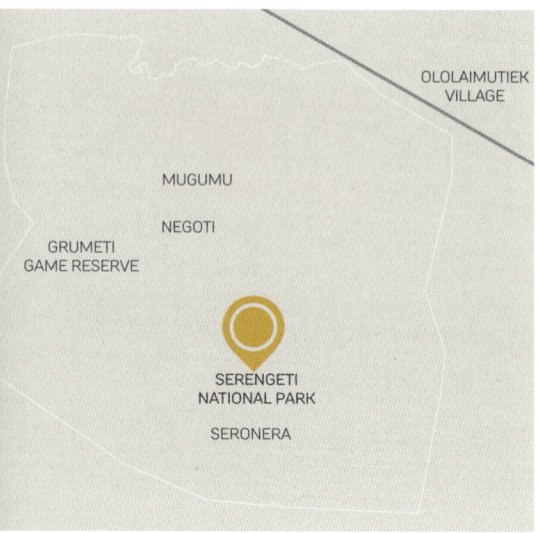

OLOLAIMUTIEK VILLAGE

MUGUMU

NEGOTI

GRUMETI GAME RESERVE

SERENGETI NATIONAL PARK

SERONERA

Serengeti National Park, Tanzania.

NAMIB DESERT

NAMIBIA

Whilst the shifting sands of this remarkable desert continue to form eye-catching dune structures, the desert as a whole remains as it has done for 55 million years. Taking its name from the Nama language word for "vast", the Namib stretches just over 1,000 miles along Namibia's coast, encroaching into South Africa to the south and Angola to the north. Coastal winds have caused the red sands to heap into awe-inspiring dunes of phenomenal size. The Big Daddy dune stands 1,066 feet tall making it the same height as the Eiffel Tower, yet it is dwarfed by the Namib's highest dune, Dune 7, which at 1,257 feet in height is more than four times as tall as the Statue of Liberty.

Receiving less than half an inch of rain annually, the Namib is desperately dry. Such a hostile environment calls for the most extreme and ingenious adaptions. The Kokerboom or quiver tree, for example, voluntarily kills off its branches to survive during extreme drought, whilst prehistoric *Welwitschia* plants spawn just two leaves but can live in excess of 1,200 years. Many of the Namib's sparse population of flora and fauna rely for survival on the sea fog that drifts into the interior and forms a heavy morning dew on occasion.

HENTIESBAAI

NAMIBIA

WINDHOEK

NAMIB-NAUKLUFT
NATIONAL PARK

REHOBOTH

MARIENTAL

Namib Desert, Namibia.

OKAVANGO DELTA

BOTSWANA

Anywhere described as "Africa's last Eden" must be an extraordinary place, and this giant yet ever-changing alluvial fan is aptly described. It is formed from the seasonal floodwaters of the Okavango river – southern Africa's third largest - on its journey from the Angolan highlands into the Kalahari Desert, creating a rare type of delta system; one that never reaches the sea.

Forming an oasis in an otherwise arid region, the delta with its swamps, lily-covered lagoons, and papyrus reed beds comprises one of the largest remaining wetland wildernesses in the world. These are remarkable for their scale (between 2,300 and 5,800 square miles in area depending on water flow) and the profusion of life they support.

More than 450 species of bird, 80 species of fish, and 1,000 species of plants including mokolwane palms, acacia and sycamore fig can be found within its boundaries whilst its nutrient-rich waters attract over a quarter of a million large mammals. Water buffalo, wildebeest, and red lechwe, the latter numbering in excess of 60,000, thrive in the delta and provide prey for some of Africa's big cats including cheetahs, leopards, and lions. White and black rhinoceros can be found here as can hippopotamus, crocodiles, and African elephants, making a veritable viewing feast for wildlife lovers.

Wildlife in the Okavango Delta, Botswana.

Aerial view of the Okavango Delta, Botswana.

Lily covered lagoon within the Okavango Delta, Botswana.

PETRA

JORDAN

Built to serve well-worn trading routes, the stunning 'Rose City' has entranced millions of visitors who make the pilgrimage to this jewel in Jordan's crown. They encounter a honeycomb of homes, workshops, elaborate tombs, and grand palaces and monuments carved into the unyielding sandstone cliffs streaked and veined in strikingly colorful reds, pinks, oranges and purples.

An Arab people called the Nabataeans developed an impressively large and lucrative trading empire that extended through parts of present day Jordan, Israel, Egypt, Syria and Saudi Arabia more than 2,200 years ago. Caravans made up of more than 1,000 camels hauling spices, perfumes, precious metals and textiles travelled the region, located between the Red and Dead seas, paying the Nabataeans customs taxes and duties for using the water holes they controlled. Petra was the location of one such water hole and had been inhabited for at least eight millennia before the Nabataeans developed the area into a city that, at its peak is estimated to have held as many as 20,000 inhabitants.

Annexation by the Roman Empire at the start of the 2nd century CE, a devastating earthquake in 363 CE and a shift in trading routes conspired to hasten Petra's decline and the city was largely

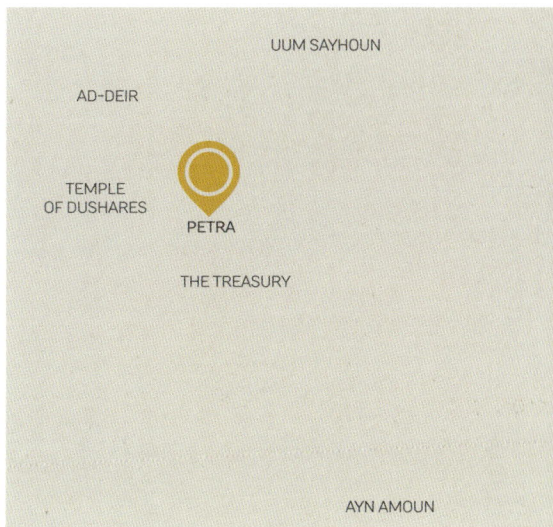

The first glimpse of Petra's Treasury (Al-Khazneh) upon exiting the passageway through al-Siq.

deserted by the 8th century. It was lost to most of the outside world for over 1,000 years until its rediscovery by Swiss explorer, Johann Ludwig Burckhardt in 1812. Disguised as a Bedouin Arab to gain entry, Burckhardt became the first modern westerner to view Petra's rock-hewn splendor and reflected, "great must have been the opulence of a city, which could dedicate such monuments to the memory of its rulers."

Access to Petra is through a sharp and, at points, claustrophobic 800-yard-long ravine, al-Siq, hemmed in by ravine walls which tower up to 600 feet above. The ravine suddenly opens out to reveal the imposing and grandiose Al-Khazneh (The Treasury). Petra's most photographed building due to its magnificent 130-foot-high façade, the building was a mausoleum and crypt built during the reign of King Aretas IV.

With motor vehicles outlawed in both al-Siq and Petra proper, visitors are able to commune with the city without noise and belching fumes. What they find is a remarkable hidden settlement with streets, temple remains and more than 500 tombs chiseled into the rock as well as a giant 8,000 capacity stone amphitheater. Looming over Petra and separated from the main city by over 800 rock cut steps is the impressive Ad-Deir Monastery with a façade even bigger and just as ornate as the Treasury.

❝ The sheer scale and majesty of this ancient city is a shock, even if you think you are prepared for it. ❞

Leigh-Ann Pow, travel journalist.

Elaborate facades line the center of Petra, thought to be the resting places of Nabataean kings. (The Tomb of the Palace).

The narrow passage of al-Siq that leads to Petra.

Close-up view of the Royal Tombs in Petra.

Looking down on Petra's Treasury (Al-Khazneh)

CHEFCHAOUEN
MOROCCO

Nestling at the base of Morocco's Rif mountains, Chefchaouen, (also known as Chaouen) was founded in 1471 as a Moorish fortress, initially for exiles from Spain. Over time, it welcomed people of other different faiths, many of them fleeing from persecution elsewhere. Arriving Jewish refugees are one theory behind the city's most picturesque feature - its many buildings, walls and doors painted blue.

Tekhelet, an ancient dye, was once used to dye ancient Jewish prayer shawls to represent god's power and according to the story, arriving Jews painted their homes in a similar color to commemorate the tradition. Competing theories state that the buildings were painted blue to keep them cool, to reflect blue as the color of optimism and happiness in Islam or to represent the city's Ras el-Maa Waterfall which supplies the city with drinking water. Whatever the origins, the outcome lends the "blue pearl of Morocco" an unusual and tranquil atmosphere, enjoyed by visitors wandering its winding narrow streets and steep alleyways. The blues throughout are far from uniform and according to Vogue travel writer, Kathryn Romeyn, Chefchaouen, "should be called the 50 Shades of Blue City, as it's full of so many variations on a theme. Powder blue, cyan, robin's-egg, indigo, cobalt, azure, periwinkle—it's painted in an endless array of shades that make it feel truly alive."

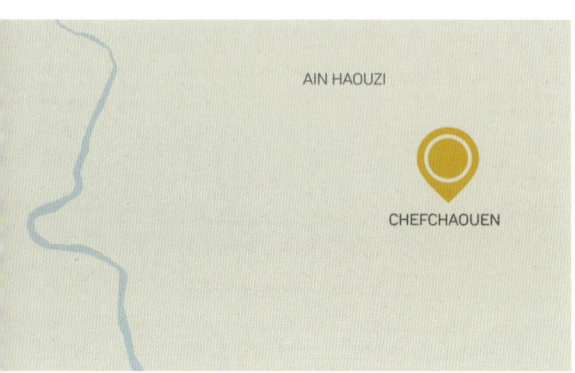

AIN HAOUZI

CHEFCHAOUEN

The mountainous landscape surrounding Chefchaouen village, Morocco.

A traditional door in the 'blue pearl of Morocco', Chefchaouen.

A colorful array of hand-crafted rugs and blankets.

A typical street in Chefchaouen, painted in traditional blue colors.

Rice field terraces in Chiang Mai, Thailand.

ASIA

CAMBODIA / CHINA / JAPAN / VIETNAM / INDIAN OCEAN / THAILAND / BHUTAN
/ INDIA / NEPAL / UZBEKISTAN / MYANMAR

ANGKOR WAT

CAMBODIA

This magnificent collection of temples, buildings, and sculptures were built in the 12th century on the orders of Khmer ruler, Suryavarman II as a Hindu place of worship but later became sacred to followers of Buddhism. Constructed largely out of sandstone blocks quarried 30 miles away and ferried down the Siem Reap River on wooden rafts, reports maintain that it took the work of 300,000 men aided by 6,000 elephants to construct the complex.

The center of the Khmer Empire for over 500 years, Angkor's major religious temple complex is enclosed by a 15 feet high sandstone wall and 620 feet wide moat crossed by a causeway. Inside, visitors are greeted by a bewildering array of galleries, platforms, temples and towers shaped like lotus buds. These all culminate in the Central Sanctuary, reached by steep steps, which rises 213 feet up. Beautiful stone sculptures and statues can be found throughout the temple complex which also features over 12,900 square feet of stunning stone wall carvings depicting scenes of battles and gods from ancient Hindu epic stories as well as more than 2,000 stone female cloud and water spirits called apsaras.

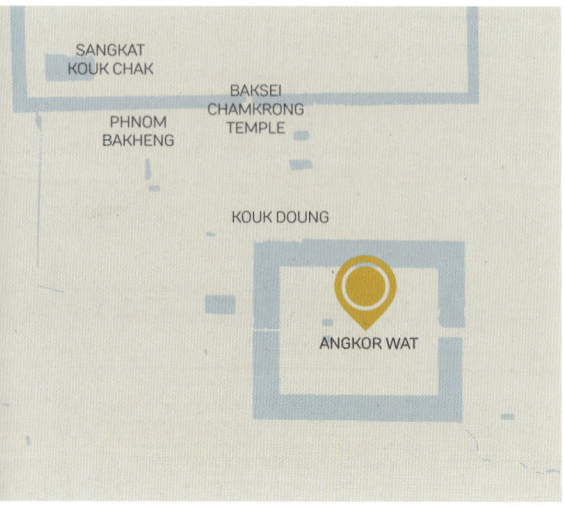

SANGKAT
KOUK CHAK

BAKSEI
CHAMKRONG
TEMPLE

PHNOM
BAKHENG

KOUK DOUNG

ANGKOR WAT

Angkor Wat temple.

After Angkor was sacked by invading Siamese forces in 1431, the complex, though remaining sacred to Buddhists, fell into disrepair. Extensive restoration, first prompted by Frenchman Henri Mouhot in 1860 and overseen by various French and international bodies, has returned it to more than a fraction of its former glory. Today more than two million visitors flock to the temple complex each year. In 2015, travel publishing company, Lonely Planet, placed Angkor as number one in its list of the top 500 global travel destinations, calling it, "a literal representation of heaven on earth".

Angkor Wat is far from the only stunning religious structure in the immediate area. Bayon Temple, built by Buddhist king Jayavarman VII, is renowned for its incredible collection of 54 towers containing 216 large sculpted faces carved into the stone, as well as more than three quarters of a mile of bas relief sculptures incorporating more than 11,000 figures all represented in stone. Travelers also make a bee line to Ta Prohm, arguably the most atmospheric of all Cambodia's temples where centuries of decay and verdant tree and moss growth gives the appearance of the temple's towers, closed courtyards and narrow corridors being swallowed whole by the surrounding dense jungle. One such tree, known as the Crocodile Tree, starred in a scene from the original *Tomb Raider* movie featuring Angelina Jolie. Cambodians remain justly proud of Angkor Wat which is the only historic temple to adorn a national flag in the world.

" Angkor Wat is of such extraordinary construction that it is not possible to describe it with a pen, particularly since it is like no other building in the world. It has towers and decoration and all the refinements which the human genius can conceive of. "

António da Madalena, a Portuguese Dominican friar who became the first European to visit Angkor in 1586.

Beautiful carvings and bas reliefs of Banteay Srei Temple, Angkor Wat.

Delicately carved Aspara dancers, Angkor Wat Temple.

The tree roots growing out of the ruins are a distinctive feature of the Ta Prohm temple.

Forbidden city, Beijing

Bronze lion in front of the Gate of Supreme Harmony within the Forbidden City, Beijing.

FORBIDDEN CITY
CHINA

Home to the last 24 emperors to rule China and a lavish reminder of the country's imperial past, it is said that a million workers labored on this mighty citadel and palace complex for 14 years during the Ming Dynasty. Completed in 1420 CE, the walled city within the heart of Beijing measures 3,153 feet by 2,470 feet and contains 980 surviving buildings, the magnificent Hall of Supreme Harmony being the largest and capable of holding 100,000 people. Most are painted in traditional vermilion red with yellow glazed tiles forming their roofs.

The world's largest collection of ancient wooden structures is a triumph of design along the principles of Yin and Yang. The complex is aligned along a north–south axis with major entrances facing south to avoid the malign Yin spirits that hail from the north. Odd numbers, associated with Yang, abound in the palace's design from the five marble bridges that cross the Golden Water to reach the Gate of Supreme Harmony to the 81 golden studs (9x9 as the number nine symbolized supremacy and eternity) that adorn its doors. Closed off from ordinary people for more than 500 years, millions now flock to the Forbidden City and its Palace Museum, home to over 1.8 million pieces of extraordinary art.

Detail of the Nine-Dragon Wall at the Forbidden City, Beijing.

WULINGYUAN SCENIC AREA

HUNAN, CHINA

Zhangjiajie National Forest Park became China's first park of this kind in 1982 and this 11,900 acre reserve is now part of this much larger conservation region in Hunan Province.
Whilst blessed with plenty to admire including picturesque brooks and valleys, the area's most famous features are its 3,000 rock stacks, most made of quartz-sandstone rising up like razor-edged fingers or spires from the valleys' floors. Some exceed 600 feet in height whilst others totter at dizzying angles that seem to defy gravity. Frequently topped with dense bursts of trees, they appear like something from another world and are said to have inspired the Hallelujah Mountains in *Avatar*.

Increasing tourist numbers to this alien place saw China match the bizarre natural landscape with two controversial but equally unusual visitor aids. The world's longest (1,410 feet) and highest (980 feet) glass pedestrian bridge spans Zhangjiajie Grand Canyon, whilst the hair-raising Hundred Dragons Elevator, at 1,070 feet, the tallest outdoor lift in the world, travels up the side of one sandstone cliff to give thrilling views of the standout "Soldiers Gathering Together" stack without requiring an arduous two hour trek beforehand.

HUANGHUAXI

SHUIRAOSIMEN

LUOMAYA

WULINGYUAN
SCENIC AREA

Zhangjiajie National Forest Park at sunset, Wulingyuan, Hunan, China.

A geisha in traditional dress creates a timeless scene, walking amongst the bamboo groves

Sunlight filters through the canopy of the tall bamboo canes.

SAGANO BAMBOO FOREST

KYOTO, JAPAN

Found in the Arashiyama district of Kyoto - one of Japan's most historic and aesthetically enjoyable cities - this dense thicket of fast-growing bamboo trees is a haven of peace and tranquillity. It spans an area of 3,950 acres with a winding pathway cut through the forest and shored up by a low, natural stone wall and simple fencing made of grasses and bamboo cane in places. The walk may only take a short time to complete but the experience is likely to stay with you for far longer.

The packed bamboo trunks and dense canopy allow dappled light and ever-changing shadows to decorate the path, accompanied by the sounds of wind causing the bamboo to bend and creak, the trunks to knock together, and the leaves to rustle. This bamboo chorus was deemed so distinctive, it has been recorded by the Japanese government as one of the 100 official Soundscapes of Japan.

A popular walk and bike ride with both local people and tourists, extremely early risers are greeted with the possibility of completing their passage through this supremely peaceful glade with only the rustling leaves for company. Just outside the forest is Tenryū Shiseizen-ji, one of Kyoto's most stunning and important Buddhist temples and a UNESCO World Heritage site since 1996.

Jojakko-ji Shrine temple in Arashiyama bamboo forest, Kyoto, Japan.

ARASHIYAMA GENROKUZANCHO

SAGANO BAMBOO FOREST

MATSUMUROKITAMATSUOYAMA

REED FLUTE CAVES

GUILIN, CHINA

Just a short, three mile taxi ride from downtown Guilin City lies this underground wonderland carved into a strata of limestone karst landscape. Hundreds of thousands of years of water erosion and acid attack on the limestone have resulted in this 788-foot-long cave filled with astonishing rock formations. Giant stalactites dangle from its ceiling, broad, rippling stone curtains line its walls and carbonate deposits have created many weird and wonderful looking rock patterns and structures, some atmospherically named including Dragon Pagoda Mushroom Hills, Fish Tail Peak and Rose Dawn over Lion Peaks. One grotto within the cave, named the Crystal Palace of the Dragon King, is big enough to hold approximately 1,000 people.

A popular misconception is that the cave gets its name from its mouth which is shaped like a flute. It is actually named after the reeds that grew in abundance just outside its entrance halfway up Bright Moon Hill and were once used to make simple flutes by local craftspeople. Ink inscriptions and poems found deep inside the caves date back to the Tang Dynasty that ruled China between 618 and 907 CE. Since that period, it has been used as a place of refuge in wartime but today is illuminated in a multi-colored light show that highlights the caves' extraordinary beauty and why it is known locally as the Palace of Natural Arts.

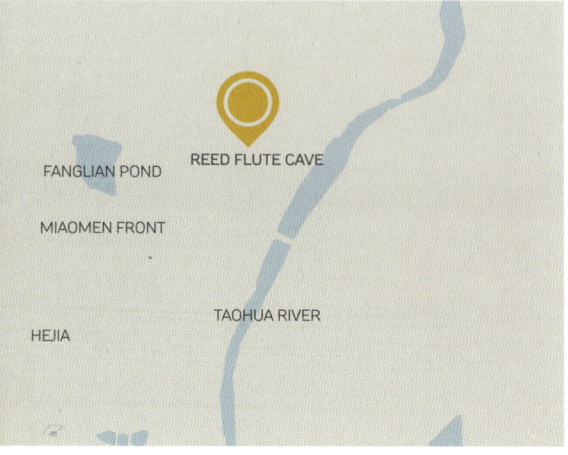

FANGLIAN POND

REED FLUTE CAVE

MIAOMEN FRONT

TAOHUA RIVER

HEJIA

This grotto, the Crystal Palace of the Dragon King, is large enough to hold 1,000 people.

SA PA
VIETNAM

Lying close to north-western Vietnam's border with China, this mountainous region has been inhabited for centuries and contains Fan Si Pan – at 10,312 feet, the highest point in south-east Asia and known as "the Roof of Indochina". French colonists established a hill station here which has grown into the quiet mountain town of Sa Pa whilst smaller villages such as Ban Ho and Ta Phin are dotted throughout the mountain range. Visitors seek these settlements out on long highland hikes and treks and to view the spectacular scenery.

Centuries of intensive agricultural practice, particularly rice farming, has resulted in sublime stacked tiers of terraced paddy fields cut and shored up on the hills' sides and layered up the slope. The field boundaries follow the sweeping lines of the undulating contours of the hills to produce a visual feast, often enhanced in allure by being cloaked in a fine mist. The arrival of rains in May and June signal "the water pouring season," and the start of the cycle of rice planting and growing on its highly attractive terraces which turn yellow in September and October as the rice gets close to harvest.

Left: Sunlight illuminating the rice terraces through storm clouds in the mountainous Sa Pa region, Vietnam.

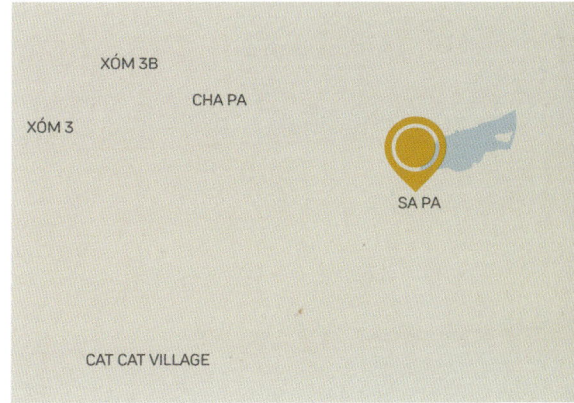

XÓM 3B

CHA PA

XÓM 3

SA PA

CAT CAT VILLAGE

RED SEA REEF
INDIAN OCEAN

A 1,400-mile-long inlet of the Indian Ocean that separates northern Africa from the Middle East and Asia, the Red Sea has been sailed and explored since antiquity. Now dotted with holiday resorts along parts of the coast, its waters contain incredible bounty. Whilst the sea reaches a depth of 9,970 feet at its deepest point, much of its waters are far shallower and the coastlines boast more than 1,200 miles of shallow fringing reefs. Many are 5,000–7,000 years old and packed full of both stony and soft corals in a kaleidoscopic riot of colors.

The coral and warm waters help support a genuine abundance of marine life, first popularized by professional divers such as Hans Hass and Jacques Cousteau. These include 1,200 species of fish, many of which are commonly found in reefs like Elphinstone and Daedalus as well as Egypt's vibrant Ras Mohammad marine park. More than 100 of these species are found nowhere else on Earth including the jet black Springer's dottyback, the surreally-attired Picasso triggerfish, and the brilliantly-colored Red Sea flasher wrasse with its electric blue veins. Divers and snorkelers are often treated to incredible technicolor displays within arm's length as well as surprise appearances of manta rays and 32 foot long whale sharks.

EGYPT

SAUDI ARABIA

RED SEA REEF

SUDAN

ERITREA

YEMEN

Divers see the best views of the Red Sea's vivid coral reefs.

The clear water allows sunlight to illuminate the reef's hard corals and colorful fish.

The Red Sea's colorful corals and schools of fish.

LI RIVER

CHINA

The 52-mile stretch of incredibly scenic winding river that links the settlements of Guìlín and Yángshuò in northeastern China is one of the most travelled by tourists and with very good reason. Its stunning karst landscape looks more like a particularly imaginative painting than a real-life landscape. Teardrop-shaped cliffs and striking limestone humps and hills mix with clumps of laurel and other trees and bamboo thickets alongside rows of waterlogged rice paddies and farm fields. There, local farmers grow sorghum, pumpkins, sesame, and sugar cane amongst other crops, often accompanied by water buffalo wallowing in the water's shallows.

An inspiration for many centuries of Chinese watercolorists and other artists, many of the thousands of limestone hills that flank the river have been given atmospheric names from Elephant Trunk Hill to Solitary Beauty Peak which is thought to represent a goddess all alone. Folded Brocade Hill is said to resemble the sweeping lines and folds of a pile of colorful silk fabric. Close by are popular detours from the main river including its highly attractive tributary, the Yùlóng River, and dozens of large caves including the majestic seven-and-a-half-mile-long Crown Cave with its own underground river.

The traditional method of fishing with cormorants is still practiced on the Li River. The mist-shrouded hills make an atmospheric backdrop.

ERTANGXIANG

DAXUZHEN

YANSHAN

YANSHANZHEN

HUIXIANZHEN

LIJIANG RIVER (LI RIVER)

CAOPINGXIANG

DABUXIANG

LIUTANGZHEN

YANGDIXIANG

NANBIANSHANXIANG

The Khuha Kharuehat Pavilion, inside the Phraya Nakhon cave, is brightly sunlit only at certain times of day.

PHRAYA NAKHON CAVE

KHAO SAM ROI YOT NATIONAL PARK, THAILAND

Khao Sam Roi Yot was Thailand's first coastal nation park, founded in 1966, and holds many treasures amongst them this extraordinary cave. It does not give its secrets away easily and is reached via a 45 minute drive from Hua Hin, followed by a walk past a secret, secluded beach, Laem Sala, and then a 1,400-foot hike-cum-climb.

The cave possesses numerous stalactites and other weird and wonderful cave formations typical of limestone caves but it is the holes in the roof which transform the cave into a truly magical destination. Bright shafts of sunlight stream in enabling lush vegetation to grow and, at certain points in the day, naturally illuminate a stunning temple constructed on a raised mound on the cave floor.

Simple, elegant and very beautiful, the Khuha Kharuehat Pavilion shines like a beacon. It was built in Bangkok for the visit of King Chulalongkorn (also known as Rama V) to the region in 1890 and then assembled on site. Subsequent Thai monarchs have also made the journey to this simple yet splendid temple in its dramatic setting and left their royal signatures clearly viewable on the cave walls.

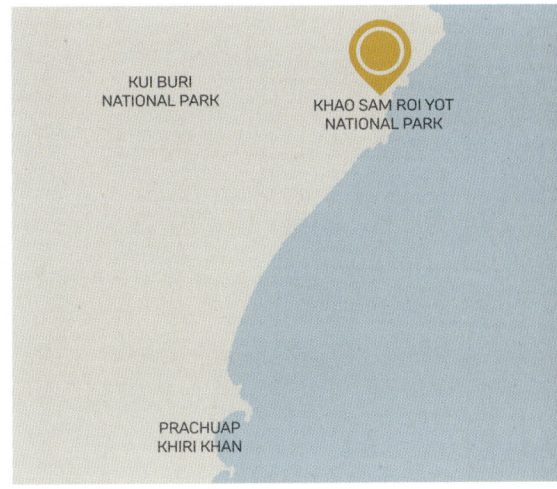

KUI BURI
NATIONAL PARK

KHAO SAM ROI YOT
NATIONAL PARK

PRACHUAP
KHIRI KHAN

TIGER'S NEST
BHUTAN

The tiny and mysterious mountainous kingdom of Bhutan is barely known to the outside world. Thirty-seven US states boast a larger area than this diminutive yet fiercely independent kingdom located in the eastern Himalayas. Paro Taktsang, or the Tiger's Nest, is Bhutan's most widely-celebrated attraction and also one of its most dramatic and striking. This Buddhist monastery was originally built in 1692 to honor Padmasambhava (also known as Guru Rinpoche) believed responsible for spreading Buddhism through Bhutan in the 700s CE. It is said that on arriving in the region, he was raised to this point high in the cliff above the Paro valley by a flying tigress before meditating in a cave there for many months.

Clinging precariously to the cliff over 3,000 feet above the floor of the valley below, the Tiger's Nest involves an arduous two-hour ascent before it can be reached by a bridge covered in prayer flags. The monastery itself consists of four main temples with golden roofs and other buildings, all connected by staircases carved into the cliff face and with balconies offering outstanding views across Bhutan and of the vertiginous drop below. The monastery also contains eight caves, one of which, Pel Phuk, is thought of as where Padmasambhava actually meditated. Monks today are required to live and meditate in these caves.

TIGER'S NEST

THIMPHU

SEMTOKHA

PARO   JAZHIPANG

HA

SAKENHAG

SANGKARI

SHARI

Plastic makeshift stupas add color to the magnificent Tiger's Nest Monastery Trail in Bhutan.

A section of the intricately carved wall at Taktsang Palphug Monastery (also known as the Tiger's Nest).

The Tiger's Nest perches high among the rocks above the Paro valley in Bhutan.

Cave 26, a large chaityagriha, or worship hall, has two upper stories containing elaborate sculptures and inscriptions.

Extensive rock-cut Buddhist monuments at Ajanta caves.

AJANTA CAVES
MAHARASHTRA, INDIA

In 1819, a young British cavalry officer, John Smith, out to hunt tigers with a local guide for company, made an extraordinary discovery in India's Maharashtra state, 280 miles east of Mumbai. Obscured behind heavy undergrowth was a cave full of ancient stone carvings and wall paintings hidden for over 1,000 years. Further investigations revealed another 29 caves, all carved out of a horseshoe-shaped section of cliff face made of flood basalt more than 200 feet above the Waghur river. The oldest, Cave 10 - the cave that Smith discovered - dates to the 2nd century BCE whilst the newest was completed before 600 CE.

Chiseled out of the rock by hand, each cave exhibits extraordinary architectural beauty with inner walls, columns, altars and stone galleries. Five are believed to be *chaityas* – Buddhist prayer halls which contain stupa at one end – whilst the remainder were Buddhist monasteries known as *viharas*. All are decorated in exquisite detail with hundreds of carvings and sculptures of deities, animals and figures alongside extraordinarily detailed paintings which historian William Dalyrimple labeled as, "some of the greatest art produced by humankind in any century, as well as the finest picture gallery to survive from any ancient civilization." The artworks, made from paints concocted of ground up lapis lazuli and other minerals mixed with animal bone glue and vegetable gum, still dazzle today in brilliant, intense shades of topaz, green and lotus blue.

Almost every surface of the Ajanta caves is covered with intricate sculptures, friezes, inscriptions and fresco-like paintings.

191

TAJ MAHAL

AGRA, INDIA

From its perfect proportions to its dazzling finish, the Taj Mahal is less a building to be revered for its opulence or scale of its construction and more to be enjoyed for the sheer, overwhelming splendor of this finely-chiseled white marble structure, inside and out. The building was conceived out of grief as Mughal Emperor Shahab-ud-din Muhammad Khurram, better known as Shah Jahan, mourned the death of his wife during childbirth, the Persian princess, Mumtaz Mahal in 1631 at the age of 37. Construction on what was to be a mausoleum and memorial to her began the following year and lasted well over a decade.

Located within a 42 acre garden complex beside the Yamuna River in Agra, the main mausoleum stands on an ornate marble plinth and is flanked by four 131-foot-tall minarets at each corner. It is topped with a large central marble dome rising 230 feet high to the tip of its finial. Inside, the mausoleum features an octagonal marble chamber, incredibly detailed filigree screens carved out of single blocks of marble, and *pietra dura* - intricately carved, inlaid, and colored floral designs, augmented by sparkling semi-precious stones. This perfect expression of Indo-Islamic architecture is beautiful, heartbreakingly so for the Emperor who was deposed by his son Aurangzeb, in 1658.

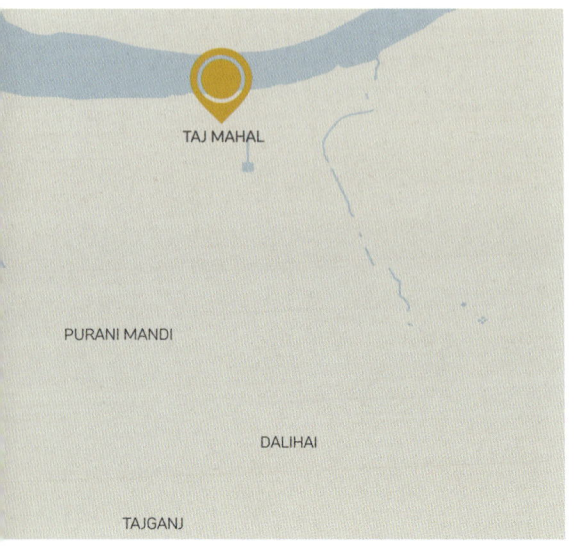

TAJ MAHAL

PURANI MANDI

DALIHAI

TAJGANJ

The Taj Mahal at sunrise.

PHI PHI ISLANDS
THAILAND

The Krabi region of Thailand possesses some of the country's most stunning landscapes, but offshore there is even more to be dazzled by. This small cluster of islands some 12 miles away from the mainland and sandwiched between Phuket and the Straits of Malacca, offers picture perfect tropical landscapes with sheer limestone cliffs and sudden, sharp rocky mountains ringed by tiny coves and impressively pristine white sand beaches. Swathes of trees blanket areas of the limestone landscape including the grey mangrove or fiery tree known as Pokok Api-Api, which originally gave the islands their name.

Surrounding the islands are the shimmering turquoise waters that make up part of Noppharat Thara-Mu Ko Phi Phi National Park. The waters in this protected region in the Andaman Sea teem with marine life from exotic corals to hawksbill turtles and cartoonish anemone clownfish. No private cars, motor scooters, or motorbikes blight the vistas obtained of the islands whose inhabitants bicycle or walk around or take traditional longtail boats to sail between destinations. Visitors from Phuket may arrive at the islands' only port on its largest island, Koh Phi Phi Don via a 45-minute speedboat ride.

Traditional longtail boats bring visitors to the crystal clear waters, white powder sand and lush tropical vegetation at Maya Bay, Phi Phi Islands.

PHUKET   KO YAO YAI   KO SRIBOYA   KO PU   PHI PHI ISLANDS   KO LANTA

RAINBOW MOUNTAINS

ZHANGYE NATIONAL GEOPARK, CHINA

A true geological wonder, these rainbow-colored rock formations, comprising mountains, ravines, towers and pillars, look as if they have been the subject of a school art project on a giant scale. Magenta, maroon, green and lemon yellow streaks of stone illuminate the prevailing vibrant deep red hues of the sandstone that forms much of these mountains, resulting in a veritable layer cake of colors that follows the undulating rise and fall of the landscape.

The mountains' story begins more than 24 million years ago with the deposition of sand, silt and minerals in the region. As these ingredients were compressed to form rock, uplifted by plate collisions and eroded, the differing minerals help create the formation's strange patterning. Chlorite and iron silicate clays, for example produce greens whilst sulfur may be responsible for the yellows found within the rock. The formation is located within Gansu province and is now protected as part of the 124 square miles of Zhangye National Geopark. Viewing boardwalks and platforms around the park direct visitors' gazes to atmospherically-named formations including Seven-Color Fan and Monks Worshipping the Buddha.

MINGYONGXIANG

GANJUNZHEN

BAIYINXIANG

ZHANGYE NATIONAL
GEOPARK

XIAOMANZHEN

LONGQUXIANG
HEPINGXIANG
DAMANZHEN

KANGLEXIANG

HEPINGXIANG

Zhangye's Rainbow Mountains really do live up to their name.

Traditional bangka outrigger boats are a familiar
sight in El Nido, Palawan.

El Nido bay and Cadlao island, Palawan, Philippines.

PALAWAN

PHILIPPINES

Palawan province is the Philippines' most sparsely-populated region and also one of its most beguiling. The province is named after the largest of its 1,780 archipelago islands which frequently tops polls for the most beautiful island destination in the world. Approaching by small traditional *bangka* outrigger boats or in more modern motor cruisers, enables visitors to experience its stunning clear, blue waters. These appear to almost merge with the rich greens of the island's mountains, which are thickly covered in verdant jungle that provides habitats for a number of endemic creatures including the Palawan flying squirrel and bearcat, as well as the smallest hoofed mammal in the world – the tiny Philippine mouse deer which stands just 7–8 inches tall at the shoulders. The mountain range runs almost the full length of the 264–mile-long island and peaks at the 6,884–foot-tall Mount Mantalingajan.

This largely unspoilt island paradise offers incredible vistas from all angles and numerous small coves, caves and other natural landmarks to explore. Located at the northernmost tip of the island, the area of El Nido is home to some 50 perfectly white sand beaches as well as scenic lagoons, limestone cliffs and offshore, stunning coral reefs protected as a marine reserve with more than 600 species of fish.

Palawan offers dramatic scenery amongst the bays and limestone cliffs.

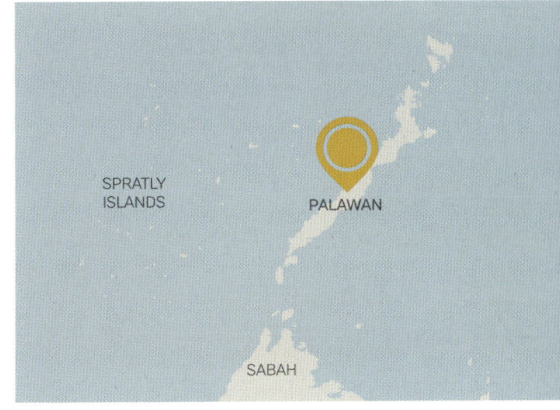

SPRATLY ISLANDS

PALAWAN

SABAH

HIMEJI CASTLE

KANSAI, JAPAN

Japan hosts numerous attractive castles and palaces, relics from earlier eras, but few are so enchantingly located as Himeji, wreathed in springtime by legions of cherry blossom trees. Built on the site of a former samurai's fortress by warlord Ikeda Terumasa in 1601, more than 20 million hours went into building this heavily fortified castle which became Japan's first UNESCO World Heritage site in 1993. The castle possesses numerous ingenious defensive features including false floors, secret compartments to hide in and *ishi-otoshi* - special chambers built to jut out over part of the castle's walls, whose floor could be retracted so that rocks and boiling oil could be dropped onto invaders scaling the walls.

Consisting of 80 buildings joined by baileys and ramparts surrounded by a 66-foot-wide moat, the castle's main building is the stone and wooden six-story *tenshukaku* or main tower. The curved, pagoda-styled roofs and whitewashed walls of the castle helped give it its nickname of White Heron Castle as it is said to look like a bird about to fly. Perched on the ends of the top roof of the main tower are two gargoyle-like sculptures of tiger fish known as *shachi gawara* - lucky charms against fire.

SHISO

NISHIWAKI

KASAI   KATO

TAKASAGO

ONO

TATSUNO

HIMEJI CASTLE

MIKI

TAKASAGO   KAKOGAWA

Spectacular sunrise at Himeji Castle.

66 The end of the ridge and the end of the world... then nothing but that clear, empty air. There was nowhere else to climb. I was standing on the top of the world. 99

Stacy Allison, the first American woman to conquer Everest, in 1988

MOUNT EVEREST
NEPAL / TIBET, CHINA

The world's tallest mountain was known as Peak 15 to the western world before it was named after a former Surveyor General of India, Sir George Everest in 1865. To the Nepalese it remains Sagarmatha or, "Goddess of the Sky" whilst to Tibetans it is known as Chomolungma meaning "Mother Goddess of the Universe."

The Himalayas (a Sanskrit name meaning "snow abode") mountain range constitutes a massive arc, some 1,500 miles long, running through portions of India, Pakistan, Afghanistan, China, Bhutan and Nepal and containing the world's third largest deposit of snow and ice after Antarctica and the Arctic. Formed through the collision of the Indian and Eurasian tectonic plates, starting 40–50 million years ago, the buckling, folding and faulting crust has resulted in a formidable barrier consisting of grand chains of lofty mountain ranges with 110 peaks with elevations greater than 24,000 feet. Everest is the tallest of all, estimated at 29,029 feet above sea level, or twenty times the height of New York's Empire State Building.

Upon seeing Mount Everest clearly for the first time in 1921 mountaineer George Leigh Mallory wrote, "It was a prodigious white fang, an excrescence from the jaw of the world. "Everest has a raw beauty with its peak possessing three main faces, north, south-west and the Kangshung or east face, meeting along pronounced ridges as well as couloirs (steep gullies) and the Yellow Band — a layer of limestone rock, below its peak.

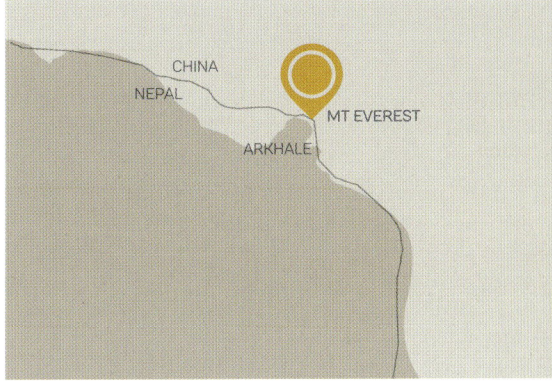

The towering North Face of Mount Everest, from North Base Camp, Tibet.

The urge to conquer Everest and reach its summit burns strongly inside every mountaineer. New Zealand beekeeper Edmund Hillary along with Nepalese Sherpa, Tenzing Norgay were the first, reaching the peak on May 29th 1953. Many have tried since but, as of 2018, fewer than 5,000 individuals have succeeded. These range in age from 13 year old Jordan Romero, from Big Bear Lake, California, in 2010, to Japanese climber Yuichiro Mirua who, in 2013, reached the summit aged 80 years and 224 days. Everest does not give up its summit lightly, however, with almost 300 climbers and guides perishing on its slopes.

Many thousands settle instead for being in the neighborhood, trekking on high altitude trails through the Himalayas, enjoying hot springs at Tatopani or on the Annapurna circuit, visiting the Ghoko valley with its six alpine lakes or travelling to the Sherpa town of Namche Bazaar. Many take their trekking to one of Everest's twin base camps, with altitudes of 16,900 and 17,598 feet.

A helpful sign points trekkers towards Mount Everest.

Colorful prayer flags surround a stupa near Dingboche village, in the Khumbu valley, Nepal, on the way to Mount Everest.

The route to Everest Base Camp is adorned by Buddhist prayer flags, here framing an evening view of the mountain from Kala Patthar.

CHOCOLATE HILLS

BOHOL, PHILIPPINES

Bohol, the Philippines' tenth largest island, harbors an unusual landscape away from its white sand beaches that fringe its coast. Deep in the island's interior lies an extraordinary collection of more than 1,260 hills, each a symmetrical cone shape. Some are slightly more rounded at their peaks but overall, they exhibit remarkable similarity. For most of the year, the grassed hills appear green but turn dark brown during the dry season giving them the distinctive color after which they were named.

Geologists believe the hills, most of which vary between 100 and 170 feet in height, were originally limestone rock formations underwater which were forced upwards by movements of the Earth's tectonic plates. The resulting outcrops were then eroded over time by rain and streams to form their smooth, rounded shapes. Local mythology, however, portrays them as either the scattered wreckage of a battle between two giants or the solidified tears of a giant called Arogo who wept at the death of a mortal woman he fell in love with.

Protected as a National Geological Monument since 1988, farmers work the flatlands between the summits, particularly cultivating rice, but the hills remain under threat from commercial interests wishing to expand a burgeoning local tourism industry or quarry the hills' limestone rock.

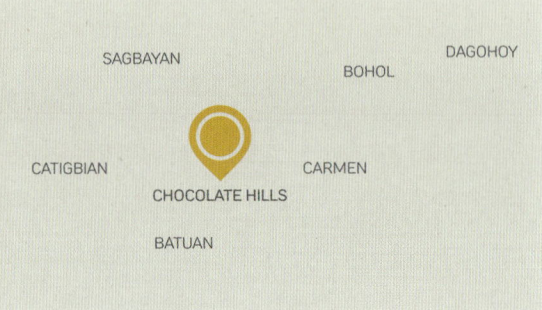

SAGBAYAN

DAGOHOY

BOHOL

CATIGBIAN

CARMEN

CHOCOLATE HILLS

BATUAN

The Chocolate Hills stretch to the horizon in Bohol, Philippines.

SAMARKAND

UZBEKISTAN

This fabled city and hub on the Silk Road trading routes of the middle ages is one of the oldest in Central Asia, founded around 2,700 years ago. Conquered by some of the most famous or infamous empire-builders in history, including Alexander the Great, Ghengis Khan and Tamerlane (also known as Timur), Samarkand was also visited by pioneering explorers such as Marco Polo and Ibn Battuta who described the city in 1333 CE as, "one of the greatest and finest of cities, and most perfect of them in beauty."

The city's attractiveness and history remain intertwined in locations such as the Shah-i-Zinda necropolis, a mazy mausoleum of grand tombs covered in exquisite blue tiles, and the monumental Bibi-Khanym Mosque, said to have been constructed by Tamerlane with the assistance of 95 elephants captured during his military campaign in the Hindustan region of India. The jewel in its crown is arguably the Registan, a square in the center of the old portion of the city bounded on three sides by large madrassahs - Islamic schools. All three: the Ulugh Beg, the Sher-Dor and the Tilya-Kori, exhibit phenomenal glazed ceramic tiles and brickwork in intricate geometric patterns.

KILACHI   DAHBED

JOMBOY

CHARHIN

KUNDUZAK
VAKHSHITEPA
SAMARKAND

The ancient Sher-Dor madrassah, on Samarkand's Registan square, is decorated with colorful tiles including unusual tiger mosaics.

MOUNT FUJI

HONSHU, JAPAN

Japan's highest mountain is also a national symbol and an inspiration for Japanese religion, art and culture. In the mind's eye, mountains are meant to be sharp, jagged, unpredictable, roughly shaped, and brooding, and often part of rugged ranges. Mount Fuji's rounded curves and standalone position above the landscape of tree-fringed lakes, sea and gently rising and falling hills, gives off an intense air of serenity and calmness. Fuji's almost symmetrical cone, capped with snow for much of the year, exudes beauty, especially during summer sunrises and sunsets when the mountain can reflect the rich light to shine a bright red.

Located around 60 miles south west of Tokyo in central Honshu, Mount Fuji is a stratovolcano, still classified as active, although its last eruption was in 1707, several weeks after the Hōei earthquake which devastated the Japanese city of Osaka. The volcano has an elevation of 12,388 feet with the slopes on its south-facing side descending down to the shore of Suraga Bay. Its base has an approximate circumference of 78 miles and rises, gently at first and then more sharply to form a crater with a diameter of over 2,600 feet which descends some 820 feet inside.

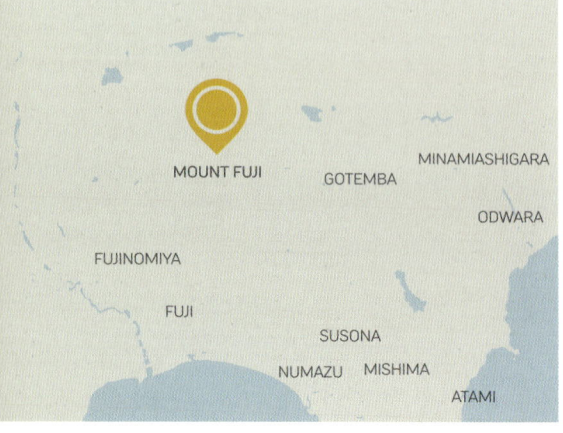

MOUNT FUJI   GOTEMBA   MINAMIASHIGARA

ODWARA

FUJINOMIYA

FUJI

SUSONA

NUMAZU   MISHIMA

ATAMI

Spring cherry blossom at the Chureito Pagoda, with Mt Fuji on the skyline.

Volcanic action from Fuji's historic eruptions helped form a partial ring of five lakes: Kawaguchiko, Saiko, Yamanakako, Shojiko and Motosuko, all renowned for their great beauty and a mecca for artists and photographers intent on creating attractive scenes with the mountain as a backdrop.

Sacred to many different sects and religions in Japan, Mount Fuji (or Fujisan as it is commonly called in Japan) has long inspired poets and artists for many, many centuries. Amongst the most famous are Taikan Yokoyama who created over 1,000 paintings of Mount Fuji during his lifetime, as well as Katsushika Hokusai who produced over 140 woodblock artworks of the calm, unchanging mountain juxtaposed and contrasted by the bustling chaos of everyday life and the ever-changing character of nature's seasons and cycles.

Mount Fuji dominates the view from Kawaguchiko lake, Japan.

Contrasting the lush green of the terraced tea fields, Mount Fuji's summit remains snow-capped for much of the year.

"With your mind as high as Mt Fuji you can see all things clearly. And you can see all the forces that shape events; not just the things happening near to you."

Miyamoto Miyashi, 16th century swordsman, Samurai and writer.

A winter view of snowy Mount Fuji clearly shows its volcanic crater.

BAGAN

MANDALAY, MYANMAR

Truly extraordinary vistas are offered at Myanmar's jewel in its crown, especially at sunrise when dramatic layers of haze reflect the sun's reddish glow and backlight the silhouettes of the many buildings that sprawl across the plain. From 1044 until 1287 when a combination of natural disasters and invading Mongol forces overturned the state, Bagan was the spiritual and economic capital of the Pagan Kingdom.

Thousands of pilgrims and scholars flocked to the region which experienced an incredible period of concentrated construction with more than 10,000 monasteries, pagodas and temples built in close proximity to each other. Some 2,200 still survive to this day — the biggest collection of Buddhist buildings in the world. Some are little stupas not bigger than a one room house, but others such as Ananda Temple and the 66m tall Thatbyinnyu Temple soar many storys high.

Visitors to the Bagan Archaeological Zone have a choice of exploring by bicycle, pedal-powered or electric, or traveling back in time by touring the zone in a horse and cart. Mopeds and motorbikes are banned, but hot air balloons flourish, especially between October and April, offering glorious aerial views of the distant mountains, the Irrawaddy River, and, of course, the remarkable collection of timeless religious structures rising up from the plain.

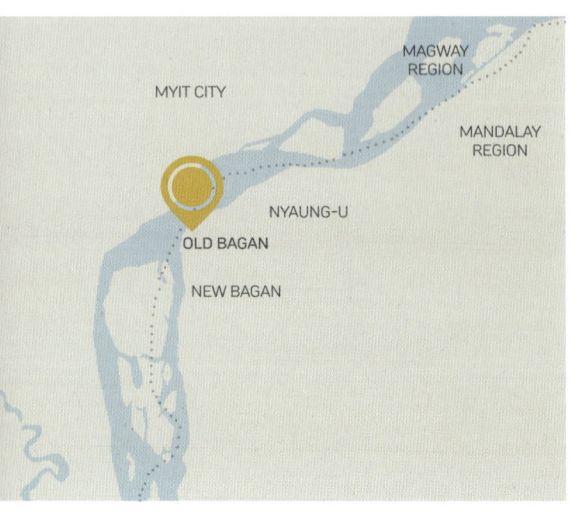

Hot air balloons take to the morning sky above the misty plain of Bagan.

Sunset at Wharanki beach, South Island, New Zealand.

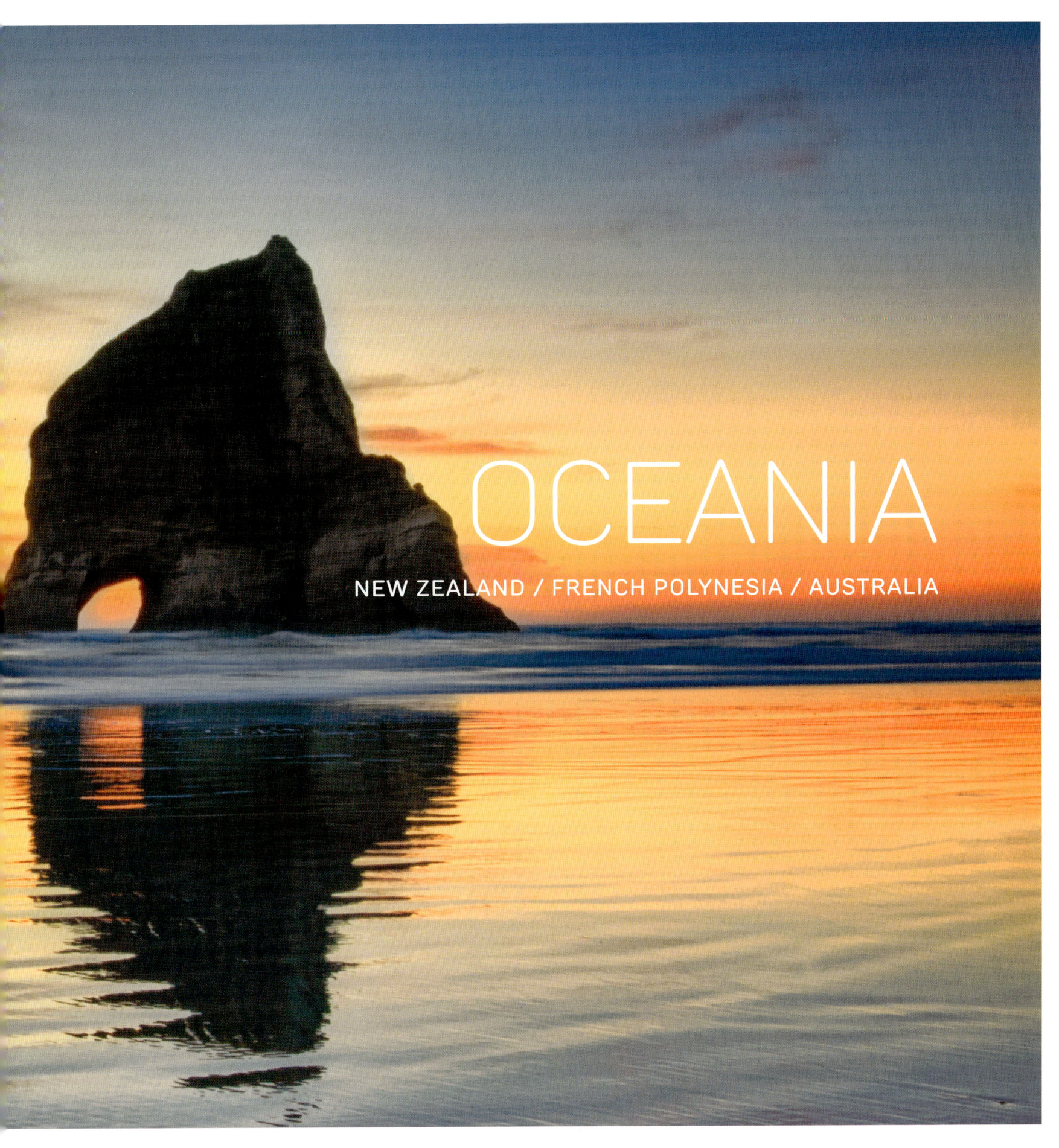

OCEANIA

NEW ZEALAND / FRENCH POLYNESIA / AUSTRALIA

ULURU

NORTHERN TERRITORY, AUSTRALIA

Towering over the surrounding landscape in Australia's Northern Territory, Uluru is an inselberg – an island mountain – which has become an Australian icon. Measuring approximately 2.2 miles long by 1.2 miles wide, Uluru rises 1,141 feet up above the surrounding plain – more than twice the height of the Washington Monument. Astonishingly, this is literally just the tip of the iceberg; the rock descends up to 8,000 feet below the surface. The formation began on a sea bed 500–600 million years ago before folding and upthrusting brought it to the surface.

Viewed up close, Uluru's surface is worn via millions of years of erosion with multitudes of gulleys, ridges and caves. Inside some of the latter are many cave paintings, sacred to local Aboriginal peoples who have inhabited the region for some 30,000 years. Surface oxidation of the sandstone rock's high iron content gives what might otherwise be a cold grey rock, a warm and remarkable orange-red hue. This coloration appears to change throughout the day depending on how light strikes the monolith, with sunsets especially notable for the vivid, dark reds

Uluru is the name given to the formation in the local Aboriginal Pitjantjatjara language but for 120 years it was known to the outside world as Ayers Rock following its discovery by William Gosse who named it after the then Chief Secretary of South Australia, Sir Henry Ayers. One hundred and twenty years later, a dual naming policy was agreed by the Australian government.

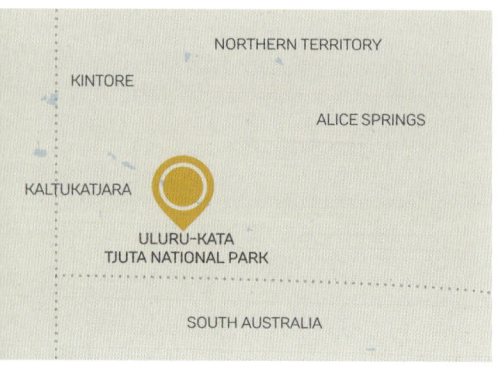

NORTHERN TERRITORY

KINTORE

ALICE SPRINGS

KALTUKATJARA

ULURU-KATA
TJUTA NATIONAL PARK

SOUTH AUSTRALIA

The footpath of the Mala walk around Uluru on a clear winters morning in the Northern Territory, Australia.

The deeply ridged sandstone rock of Uluru glowing red in the light of the sunset.

The 'island mountain' rising more than 1000 feet above the plain at Uluru Kata Tjuta national park.

BORA BORA
FRENCH POLYNESIA

Lying 165 miles northwest of Tahiti, this small group of islands lays claim to be the most picturesque in the Pacific. Verdant palm groves and dense vegetation on the slopes contrast with the dark jagged peaks of the islands' mountains and the dazzling white sand beaches that ring their shorelines. Bora Bora has been inhabited for over 1,300 years and was first landed upon by Europeans when Captain James Cook's first Pacific expedition alighted in 1769. Cook returned eight years later, but the islands were later claimed by the French as a colony.

The mountainous main island, Bora Bora, has a volcanic backstory and rises sharply to its twin peaks of Mount Otemanu (2,385 feet) and Mount Pahia (2,159 feet). Measuring just 6 miles long and 2.5 miles wide at its longest and widest points, it is surrounded by coral reefs and on its western side, close to its biggest settlement of Vaitape, harbors a large blue lagoon that, in the words of novelist James A. Michener, is "so stunning, that there are really no adequate words to describe it." Containing the smaller island of Toopua and Toopua Iti and many overwater bungalows perched on stilts, the lagoon is a natural haven for a wide array of marine life.

BORA BORA
TAHA'A
RA'IĀTEA   HUAHINE-ITI

TETIAROA

MO'OREA
MAI'AO   FRENCH POLYNESIA

Overwater bungalows on stilts dot Bora Bora's lagoon, with Mount Otemanu in the background.

GREAT BARRIER REEF

QUEENSLAND, AUSTRALIA

Stunning in its scale, beauty and biodiversity, the world's largest reef is one of the seven wonders of the natural world. It stretches an incredible 1,440 miles along the coast of the north-eastern seaboard of the Australian state of Queensland and consists of more than 3,000 individual reef systems and coral cays along with larger islands. In total, the reef spans an area half the size of Texas and as International Space Station astronauts testify, is so large it can be clearly seen from space.

Around 600 different species of coral are found in the reef's waters, coming in all shapes, colors and sizes. They provide habitats for a truly rich and stunning array of marine life including the mighty Pacific manta ray which can grow to 23 feet wide and weigh as much as a small car. The Pacific manta is just one of 133 species of rays and shark that call the Great Barrier Reef their home. They are joined by an astonishing 1,625 species of fish, 3,000 species of mollusks and 17 species of sea snakes. More than 200 species of bird visit the reef along with as many as 10,000 whales between June and September as they migrate from the Southern Ocean to the reef in order to breed.

CAIRNS

TOWNSVILLE

GREAT BARRIER REEF

MACKAY

ROCKHAMPTON

BUNDABERG

Aerial view of part of the Great Barrier Reef

The Great Barrier Reef is home to a wide variety of fish, including the Napoleon fish (humphead wrasse), which can reach more than six feet in length.

Diving and snorkeling are popular ways to see the Great Barrier Reef.

MILFORD SOUND

SOUTH ISLAND, NEW ZEALAND

Hidden away on the southwest tip of New Zealand's South Island is a magnificent fjord, just over nine miles long and bounded by near vertical cliffs rising a minimum of 3,900 feet high above its dark, inky waters in which fur seals and dolphins can sometimes be spotted frolicking. Less than 150 people live along Milford Sound mostly working in conservation or tourism, helping to welcome as many as one million visitors per year to this captivating location.

One of Oceania's wettest places, Milford Sound receives over 252 inches of rainfall per year. On particularly stormy days, a foot of rain can fall, creating a number of temporary waterfalls down the fjord's rocky walls such as the Four Sisters. Two large permanent falls also exist. Waters cascade 495 feet down the scenic Stirling Falls and 530 feet down Lady Bowen Falls, a site that since early 2018 could again be seen in close proximity following the reopening of the falls trail after a closure lasting almost two decades.

Milford Sound's highest point is named after its resemblance to a bishop's headdress. Mitre Peak soars 5,551 feet above sea level and contains five separate pinnacles closely grouped together. Behind it lies Sinbad Gully, a U-shaped valley sculpted by glacial action and where the kakapo bird, feared extinct, was rediscovered.

Called Piopiotahi in the Maori language, Milford Sound is New Zealand's best known tourist destination.

MOUNT ASPIRING

MILFORD SOUND

GLENORCHY

QUEENSTOWN HILL

GREENSTONE

QUEENSTOWN

SYDNEY HARBOUR

NEW SOUTH WALES, AUSTRALIA

Europeans came face to face with this stunning natural harbor, one of the world's finest, for the first time in 1770. A former river estuary drowned by rising water levels some 17,000 years ago, this giant 21.2 square mile haven is the hub of Sydney coastal life and an inspiring setting for events such as New Year's Eve firework displays and the Sydney to Hobart yacht race. Officially known as Port Jackson, it is dotted with countless attractive bays and inlets, small islands, and 20 beaches including the incredibly picturesque Camp Cove and Seven Shillings Beach. The harbor is also home to some 20,000 private boats and is crossed by four bridges and more than 15 million ferrygoers each year. Hundreds of restaurants, cafes and other businesses line its fringes.

From many visitors' first encounter with the harbor at Circular Quay, a major transport and cultural hub, numerous vantage points beckon. Those seeking an overview of the entire harbor might head for locations such as the Hornby Lighthouse or, up on Blue Street, the Harborview Hotel, whilst lovers of natural bushland often travel around Bradleys Head to Clifton Gardens or head out west of Manly to reach heathland and wooded groves.

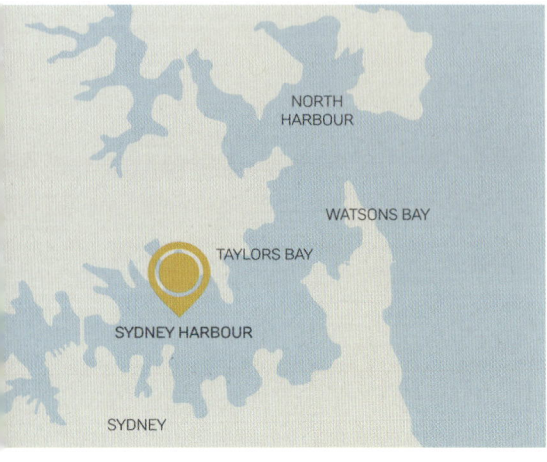

NORTH HARBOUR

WATSONS BAY

TAYLORS BAY

SYDNEY HARBOUR

SYDNEY

Sydney Opera House and Harbour Bridge at night.

The jewel in the harbor's crown is the distinctive and daring Sydney Opera House designed by Danish architect, Jørn Utzon and opened in 1973. A global icon attracting over two million visitors a year, its sail-like roof was assembled from 2,194 sections of pre-cast concrete topped by more than 1.05 million gleaming ceramic tiles. Some 580 sunken piers support the 600-foot-long building's great heft – around 790 times the weight of the Statue of Liberty. More than 1,500 shows and performances are staged each year in this structure lauded as "a masterpiece of 20th century architecture" and "a daring and visionary experiment that has had an enduring influence" by UNESCO which made it a World Heritage site in 2007.

Behind the Opera House towers the arched Sydney Harbor Bridge with a total length of 3,770 feet. Nicknamed the Coathanger, more than 52,000 tons of steel went into completing its distinctive structure which was viewed by over a million people attending its opening in 1932. Rising 440 feet above the harbor waters, it dominates parts of the skyline as, in the words of American travel writer Bill Bryson, "you can see it from every corner of the city, creeping into frame from the oddest angles, like an uncle who wants to get into every snapshot."

Sydney Opera House with Sydney Harbour Bridge in the background, Queensland, Australia.

Sydney Opera House is an iconic piece of modern architecture, and probably the most recognizable feature on the Harbour's shoreline.

Detail of internal space in the Sydney Opera House.

"Sydney is rather like an arrogant lover... when the sun comes out, it bats its eyelids, it's glamorous, beautiful, attractive, smart, and it's very hard to get away from its magnetic pull."

Baz Luhrmann, movie director

FRED HOLLOWS

A Sydney Harbour ferry boat docked at Milsons Point on the North Shore, with a view to the Opera House.

THE TWELVE APOSTLES

VICTORIA, AUSTRALIA

At the end of World War I, Australian soldiers returning home constructed a 151-mile road running along the south coast of Victoria from Torquay to Allansford in memory of their fallen colleagues. Completed in 1932, the Great Ocean Road is not only the world's largest war memorial, it is also a marvelously scenic coastal route through rainforest, along cliffs and past some of southern Australia's greatest natural landmarks – from the Loch Ard Gorge and London Arch to Bell's Beach, a prime surfing spot.

Three quarters of the way along the road from Torquay, lies the road's most powerful and famous feature. The Twelve Apostles were originally named the Pinnacles and then, the Sow and Pigs. This series of rock stacks stand just offshore and are the results of the endless pounding of the limestone cliffs by the unceasing sea, which formed caves that were eroded further to form arches and then stacks over a period of 10 to 20 million years. The process is ongoing as witnessed by the loss of one of the eight remaining Apostles in 2005, with the 165-foot-tall stack crumbling into the sea.

A spectacular view of the Twelve Apostles at sunset, Great Ocean Road, Victoria, Australia

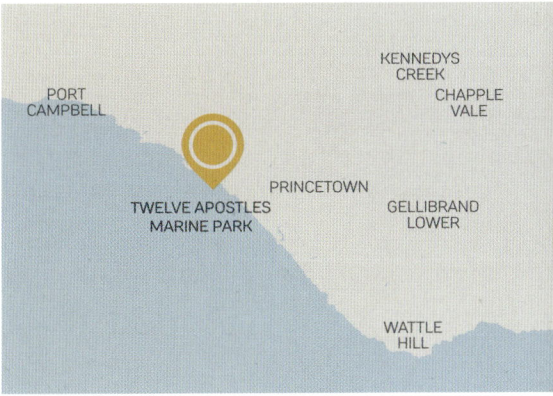

LAKE TEKAPO

SOUTH ISLAND, NEW ZEALAND

The 'most Instagramed location in New Zealand' is one of a series of three lakes, running roughly in parallel in the South Island's MacKenzie Basin and all reachable via a series of attractive hiking trials. Lake Tekapo gets its name from its original discoverers, the Maori and covers an area of 32 square miles. Rock flour (finely ground rock) from glacial action in the waters gives the lake a distinct milky turquoise coloration, in contrast to the lush, golden tussock grass that surrounds much of the lake and the dark brooding hills and snow-capped mountains of New Zealand's Southern Alps in the distance to the north.

Some three hours away by car from Christchurch, the lake and its surroundings possess a rugged attractiveness, enhanced in early December when vast tracts of colorful lupin flowers come into bloom around its shore. The area also possesses some of the clearest skies imaginable and has been designated one of the world's first four Dark Sky Reserves. The absence of light pollution means one can gaze up into the night sky and clearly view thousands of stars from the Milky Way and, occasionally, the spectacular light show of Aurora Australis – the Southern Lights.

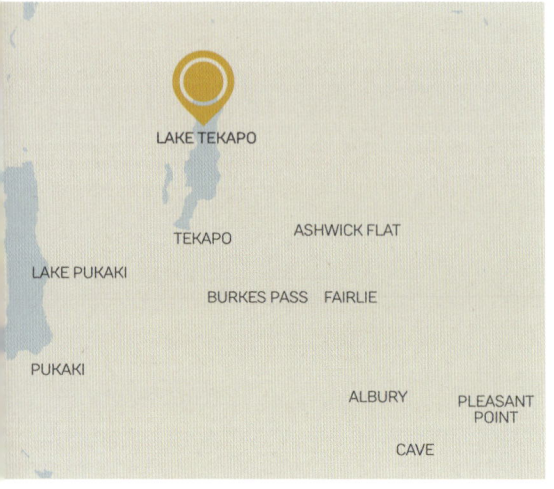

LAKE TEKAPO

TEKAPO   ASHWICK FLAT

LAKE PUKAKI

BURKES PASS   FAIRLIE

PUKAKI

ALBURY   PLEASANT POINT

CAVE

The Milky Way galaxy clearly visible in the night sky above the Church of the Good Shepherd, Lake Tekapo, New Zealand.

View from the Mount John Observatory, Lake Tekapo.

Each summer, swathes of colorful lupins flower alongside the lake.

The frozen antarctic landscape.

ANTARCTICA

ANTARCTICA

Larger than the United States and Mexico combined, and the world's coldest, driest, and windiest continent, Antarctica is also the most isolated and least populated landmass on Earth. People are drawn to its unique qualities, its untouched pristineness and its stark, brutal beauty – from imposing ice floes and icebergs to towering mountains, vast glaciers, craggy crevasses, and a surprisingly rich array of wildlife that lives around its coastal fringes, including 15 species of whales, Weddell, and leopard seals, and the continent's iconic penguins, only two species of which — emperor and Adélie — live on the main continental landmass.

The 2,200-mile-long Transantarctic Mountain Range splits the continent into two regions: a larger eastern region and the western region which includes the Antarctic Peninsula. This peninsula extends 810 miles northwards towards South America and is covered in mountains including the continent's highest point, the peak of the Vinson Massif, standing 16,050 feet tall. Ninety -eight percent of the land mass is covered in an ice sheet that extends to an astonishing depth of up to 13,000 feet in places and holds 90 percent of the world's freshwater reserves according to the British Antarctic Survey. Hidden below the ice are more than 400 subglacial lakes, the largest of which, Lake Vostok, covers 4,830 square miles, making it larger than Jamaica.

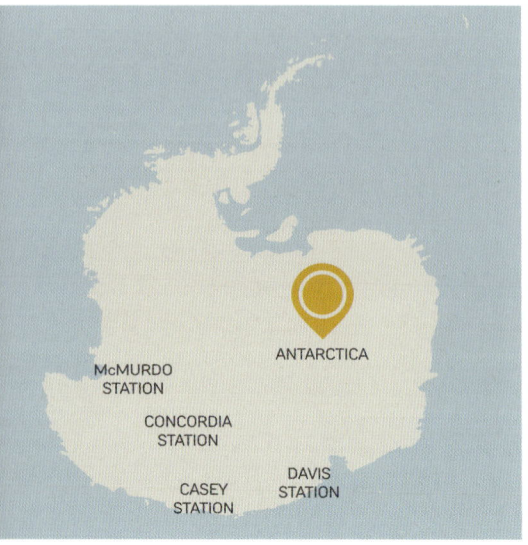

ANTARCTICA

McMURDO STATION

CONCORDIA STATION

CASEY STATION

DAVIS STATION

Braving the inhospitable climate, tourists take a Zodiac boat to get close to a glacier.

Undiscovered until the 19th century, the continent lacks permanent settlements but does feature some 70 research and scientific stations, comprising a 1,000-strong population in winter when the sun sets in April and doesn't re-emerge until mid-August. Numbers rise up to 10,000 in the Antarctic summer and are swelled further by polar tourists arriving by cruise ship, craving the chance to walk in former polar explorers' footsteps. Located on the southern tip of Ross Island, America's McMurdo Station is the largest base in the Antarctic region, housing 1,250 people at peak habitation and reliant on an annual restocking when some 11,000 million pounds of food and other supplies are shipped in. Another US station, Scott-Amundsen, lies beside the South Pole, where twelve flags are flown in a circle to commemorate the twelve nations who signed the landmark treaty of cooperation in 1959 to keep Antarctica demilitarized and free of commercial exploitation of resources.

The islands relatively close to Antarctica also offer considerable bounty. Zavodovski in the South Sandwich Islands, for example, is home to two million chinstrap penguins – the world's largest penguin colony, James Ross Island has caches of prehistoric fossil finds whilst Deception Island is a land of fire and ice – an active volcano with a flooded caldera and much geothermal activity.

A tourist Zodiac boat is dwarfed by the scale of the Antarctic glaciers.

A Weddell seal in the Antarctic peninsula.

Visitors travel in an old research ship to admire the Antarctic landscape.

" Antarctica has this mythic weight. It resides in the collective unconscious of so many people, and it makes this huge impact, just like outer space. It's like going to the moon. "

Jon Krakauer, US mountaineer and writer.

An iceberg off the west coast of Antarctica.

CREDITS